The Legend That Is BUDDY HOLLY

Richard Peters

POP UNIVERSAL
SOUVENIR PRESS

First published 1990 by Souvenir Press Ltd,
43 Great Russell Street, London WC1B 3PA
and simultaneously in Canada

ISBN 0 285 63005 9

Acknowledgements

The author and publishers are grateful to the following for their help in the writing of this book: Bill Lofts, Curtis James, Alan Monk, Laurie Mansfield, Trevor Lailey of the British Buddy Holly Society and Todd Slaughter of the Official Elvis Presley Fan Club. The following newspapers and magazines have granted permission for quotations from their pages: *The Times*, *The Guardian*, *Daily Mail*, *Daily Express* and Beaverbrook Newspapers, *The Tennessean*, Nashville, *Rolling Stone*, *Record Mirror* and *New Musical Express*. The photographs are published by courtesy of the Board of Trustees of the Victoria & Albert Museum, Popperfoto, Solo Picture Agency, Topham Picture Source, The Tennessean Photo Library, Phillips (Auctioneers) Ltd., *Radio Times*, British Film Institute, Warner Brothers, Columbia Pictures, Universal Pictures, Entertainment Film Distributors and Decca Records.

Photoset in Linotron Sabon by Rowland Phototypesetting Ltd,
Bury St Edmunds, Suffolk

Printed in Great Britain by St Edmundsbury Press Ltd,
Bury St Edmunds, Suffolk

In Memory of
BUDDY HOLLY
—for the music

&
ALAN CUTMORE
—for introducing me to it

THE CRICKETS Exclusive Coral Recording Artists

COPYRIGHT

'The main thing about Buddy is that he was a good musician, that he made it on his music and not publicity or an idol type of shot. We did try and figure out what would sell so we could go out on the road and play music and not have to set ceramic tiles—which is what we were into when we started recording. It was strictly kids playing what we liked to play. Buddy had this confidence—he had a lot of charisma when he played. When I saw Elvis, I couldn't believe it. Holly had the same kind of stage presence.'

JERRY ALLISON
Drummer of The Crickets, 1986

'Even though Buddy Holly never had a Number One Single in America, his legacy is immeasurable. Holly and The Crickets established the precedent for a self-contained rock & roll band, that is, one that wrote its own material and had enough studio freedom to do what it felt, in the process bridging country and rock.'

CHET FLIPPO
Rolling Stone, September 21, 1978

'Buddy Holly, rock 'n' roll's Mozart, was a myopic, tooth-capped hero of the monochrome Eisenhower era. Since his death in 1959, having achieved more at 22 than most musicians in a generous lifetime, the world has witnessed Kennedy and the hula-hoop, Vietnam and the kaftan, a giant leap for mankind and the hot-air hand-drier, Dylan and Dallas, Thatcher and the thoughts of Chairman Mao. But Holly, ignorant of all this, has stayed perfectly still.'

JOHN COLLIS
The Guardian, 30 August, 1986

Contents

The Legend

In the early hours of 3 February, 1959, the 22-year-old American singer Buddy Holly and two fellow musicians, J. P. Richardson, 'The Big Bopper', and Ritchie Valens, died in a plane crash at Clear Lake, Iowa. Around the world, an army of rock 'n' roll fans caught their breath in disbelief and dismay . . . but if a star had died that chill winter morning, a legend, too, had been born.

Thirty years on, Buddy Holly is as firmly entrenched in the pantheon of dead show business heroes as James Dean, Marilyn Monroe and his great contemporary in the field of pop music, Elvis Presley. Buddy was not handsome like James Dean or photogenic like Marilyn Monroe, nor did he rock the world as outrageously and controversially as Elvis; yet is it as easy to name the films or records by these stars as it is to roll off the tongue the titles of Buddy Holly songs?

. . . 'That'll Be The Day', 'Peggy Sue', 'Oh Boy!', 'Everyday', 'Maybe Baby', 'Rave On', 'Heartbeat', 'Words of Love', 'True Love Ways', 'It Doesn't Matter Anymore' . . .

His music has, of course, influenced many of the super-stars of the music business, just as his fame has become the subject of books, films, television specials, memorabilia and displays of public admiration around the world. Indeed, in only the last five years the following major Holly-days have occurred:

7 September, 1986. The 50th anniversary of Buddy Holly's birth is marked by a British television spectacular featuring Jerry Allison and Joe Mauldin, the surviving members of his group, The Crickets, as well as the Everly Brothers, Paul McCartney and Keith Richard . . .

17 January, 1987. The movie *Peggy Sue Got Married*, starring Hollywood's

9

Opposite: Buddy Holly—the face of a legend.

The magic of Buddy Holly lives on: 'Fifties-style dancers in the London of the 'Eighties celebrating 'Buddy Holly Week'.

latest sex symbol, Kathleen Turner, and inspired by Buddy Holly's famous song, opens to ecstatic reviews in America and Britain . . .

3 February, 1988. Buddy Holly's death is marked in Australia by two programmes of his records, presented by Barry Bissall on Fox FM in Melbourne, and by John Pemberton on SAFM in Adelaide . . .

29 January, 1989. 'Words of Love', a dramatic television reconstruction of Buddy Holly's last hours, written by Philip Norman and starring Pancho Russell, is shown on BBC 2 . . .

3 February, 1989. 'Not Fade Away', a BBC radio programme to mark the thirtieth anniversary of Buddy Holly's death, includes interviews with Buddy's mother, his widow, and his producer, Norman Petty . . .

4 September, 1989. Relatives of Buddy Holly, Ritchie Valens and J. P. Richardson gather in Port Arthur, Texas, for the unveiling of sculptures of the rock singers 30 years after their deaths . . .

12 October, 1989. Opening night of the first major musical, *Buddy—The Buddy Holly Story*, at the Victoria Palace, London, starring Paul Hipp as Buddy . . .

23 April, 1990. A collection of Buddy Holly memorabilia is auctioned at Phillips in London and sets a record for rock nostalgia by raising £36,355 . . .

Some of the items of Holly memorabilia auctioned in London in April 1990.

Such events, and more like them elsewhere, have revealed the extent of public interest in the young Texan singer who died before his talent could reach its full potential, yet who has still left an indelible mark on our times. In an anniversary tribute in February 1986, the rock magazine, *Rolling Stone*, succinctly put it:

Although Holly's rock 'n' roll career was brief it yielded a wealth of material. 'Words of Love' inspired the Beatles (whose very name was a homage to the Crickets) and 'Not Fade Away' provided the Rolling Stones with their first British Top Ten hit. Holly's approach suggested the shape of rock to come: he wrote his own material, exploited studio technology and employed the now classic line-up of two guitars, bass and drums. In a short span of time, Buddy Holly created music that was timeless.

All of The Beatles, for instance, have acknowledged their debt to Buddy. Some years ago John Lennon explained how, in 1959, when the group were about to get their first important audition, they were desperately casting around for a name.

'I was sitting at home one day,' said John, 'just thinking about what a good name the Crickets would be for an English group. We'd all been fans of Buddy Holly and the Crickets. We particularly liked the Crickets bit because it had a nice double meaning. Then the idea of beetles came into my head. I decided to spell it BEATLES to make it look like beat music just as a joke.'

George Harrison remembers how John 'just arrived' with this name one day—and how they all agreed at once it was absolutely right. He also has another fascinating story to tell relating to Buddy Holly. It concerns the second Beatles tour of America, when an airline owner whom George refers to as 'Pigman' invited them to his ranch in Arkansas and the four boys flew from Dallas to an intermediate airport.

'Pigman met us there in a little plane with just the one wing on top and with one or maybe two engines,' he says. 'It was just so like Buddy Holly, that one, that was probably the closest we came to that sort of musicians' death. I don't mean it nearly crashed because it didn't, but the guy had a little map on his knee with a light, as we were flying along and he was saying, "Oh, I don't know where we are." And it was pitch dark and there are mountains all around and he's rubbing the windscreen trying to get the mist off. Anyway finally we found where we were and so we landed in a field with tin cans on fire to guide us in.'

Paul McCartney has perhaps the greatest admiration of all the four ex-Beatles for Buddy Holly, and in the late 'Seventies his company, MPL Productions, purchased the rights to all the songs Buddy wrote during his association with Norman Petty. He has also revealed that the very first record the Beatles made privately in Liverpool was Buddy's 'That'll Be The Day'—and he still owns the only known copy.

Although Paul obviously never met Buddy (he does, though, own a pair of cufflinks, presented to him by Norman Petty, which the singer was reputedly wearing the day he died), he has become friends with Jerry Allison and Joe Mauldin and in 1988 produced a single with them, 'T-Shirt', on which he played the keyboard. The tune by Jim Imray was the winning entry in a competition for a new song in the style of The Crickets, which had been run in conjunction with the annual 'Buddy Holly Week' which takes place from 7–14 September.

Paul himself inaugurated this festival in 1976, to coincide with Buddy's birthday and help keep his music and memory alive, and among the regular guests of honour have been the two Crickets. Held in London, the event includes concerts, a rock 'n' roll dance championship (with prizes of trips to Buddy's home town of Lubbock) and a huge party at the Lyceum attended each year by more than 2,000 fans and stars of the record world. Among the famous Holly fans who have turned up in appropriate 'Fifties clothes have been Ringo Starr, Billy Fury, Billy Connolly, Pamela Stephenson, Mel Smith and Griff Rhys Jones. McCartney himself caused the biggest sensation in September 1982 when he arrived in horn-rimmed glasses, slicked-back hair and a suit that made him look the spitting image of Buddy!

Says Paul, 'Buddy Holly has been a big influence on me and all the Beatles. When we heard what he could do, John Lennon and I decided we'd have a go at writing our own material. I've always loved his music—and I'm sure that like millions of others, I always will.'

Keith Richard of the Rolling Stones, who based his early guitar technique on Buddy Holly, has paid similar tribute.

'Buddy Holly was the start of everything,' he says. 'His music had it all.'

It is difficult—if not impossible—to define just *what is* Buddy Holly's music. Certainly his songs have simple chords and are easy to play, as well as being instantly rememberable and completely timeless. Each successive generation has

Opposite: The Crickets (*above*) were the inspiration for The Beatles—a debt all four Liverpool musicians have acknowledged.

The Beatles

found the music as fresh as if it had just been newly minted. At its most basic, what he did was take his native Texan Country and Western music, meld it with a love of black rhythm and blues, and move both styles on a step farther from their folk roots without ever losing the pioneer spirit. One critic has written that Buddy Holly 'invented pop music with balls', and if by that he means that Buddy's music is the living spirit of rock 'n' roll, then that is probably as close as anyone can, or needs, to get.

And as for the man himself, there can clearly be no doubt, as all the records, films, fan clubs, memorabilia and this book itself bear witness: the Legend that is Buddy Holly lives on . . .

Buddy Holly at 50? An imaginative sketch by David Ace of the *Evening News* to mark the thirtieth anniversary of the star's death; and the surviving Crickets in London in 1990 with Paul Hipp, star of the musical, *Buddy*.

Deep in the
Heart of Texas

The gateway to Lubbock, where Buddy Holly was born, is Dallas, that ultra-modern city of shimmering glass towers famous in TV soap opera . . . which sells postcards at its airport showing in graphic detail the Dealey Plaza where Lee Harvey Oswald shot President Kennedy in November 1963. Yet this bizarre conjunction of ostentatious wealth and people making a few bucks out of the assassination of a much loved leader is somehow the essence of Texas. Nothing, the visitor soon learns, is quite what it seems.

The same kind of contradictions one discovers in Dallas are also to be found in Lubbock, after driving 300 miles or so to the west via Abilene. For though this community of 200,000 people in the midst of the great western plains of Texas, which survives on agriculture and cotton, is probably only known to the world in general as Buddy Holly's home town, there is actually precious little sign of the fact—no civic building or park named in his memory; no street or house bearing his name.

To anyone who has visited Memphis, less than seven hundred miles away in Tennessee—which was the home of the other famous American legend, Elvis Presley, a contemporary of Buddy Holly—the contrast could not be starker. For there every house, every road, every inch that can be associated in some way with the dead rock star has been refurbished, postered and placarded into something little short of a shrine, with all the commercial paraphernalia associated with such places. But for Buddy in Lubbock, there is . . . very little indeed.

Once the visitor reaches Lubbock, the 'Hub City of the Plains', in the midst of a vast, flat plateau, it is not difficult to find one's way about: the streets are conveniently numbered 1–100 in one direction and crossed the other way by

16

letters from A–Z. Yet go to 1911, 6th Street, where the community's most famous son was born, and there is only an empty site. And at 1305, 37th Street, where he grew up, neither the present occupants nor the neighbours have heard of Buddy Holly.

Nor is there anyone to talk about him at Hutchinson Junior High which he attended as a boy, or Lubbock High School where he went as a teenager and began to develop the friendships and love of music which would be the core of his short life. The simple tombstone erected to his memory in the sprawling Lubbock cemetery is not that easy to find, either, though the guitar cut into its surface helps differentiate it from that of a Clint Beadle on one side and the final resting place of not one but two Roland Edwin Ponces, Snr. and Jnr., on the other.

In fact, it is quite possible to walk right past the grave because the name on it reads Buddy Holley—the star's real name until the 'e' was inadvertently dropped by his first recording company in 1956. The headstone is, apparently, the second one on the tomb: the first, a carved upright guitar, was stolen by some ghoul in 1959, with Buddy barely cold under the ground.

Apart from the grave, there is a seven-and-a-half foot high statue of Buddy in a typical pose strumming his guitar, which can be seen standing on a rather threadbare patch of grass by the Civic Centre, opposite a Holiday Inn. But this was erected by private subscription and not raised until 1980. And not far away the visitor will find the unprepossessing shop run by the Buddy Holly Memorial Society, which sells records and other small items of memorabilia. This is operated by Bill Griggs, a chunky figure from Connecticut, who dresses in check shirt, jeans and cowboy boots and moved to Lubbock ten years ago to do something to promote the man he calls 'my obsession'. Bill, who has named his daughter Holly, says the Society now has 6,000 members—but in 33 *other* countries.

Opposite: The statue of Buddy Holly by Utah artist Grant Speed, who is seen at the unveiling in Lubbock on 5 September, 1980. Above: the headstone which marks the last resting place of Buddy Holly, with the correct spelling of the family surname.

..... Class of '55

ROSE MARY HOLDER

NORA HOLLAND

JOHN HOLLARS

J. M. HOLLERS

BUDDY HOLLEY

STELLA HOLTON

Ringing up two of the cash registers every day in the Lubbock Senior High cafeteria are sophomore checkers Morris Scales, left, and Tommy Price, right. Verna Harrington is having her lunch tray checked.

JERRY DON HOPKINS

VAN HORN

JACK HOUSE

JAMES ROY HOWARD

JOYCE HOWARD

PAT HOWARD

STUART HUDNALL

SUE HUFSTEDLER

BOBBY HUGHEY

SUE HUMPHREY

ANN HUMPHREYS

JIMMY HUMPHREYS

CARLTON HUNEKE

MED HUNT

JIMMY HUNTER

DOUGLAS HUTTON

GLENDA INGRAM

KAY ISBELL

WAYNE JACOBS

CAROL JAMES

BONNIE JANES

GERALD JANEWAY

LANELL JENNINGS

The young Buddy Holley (*centre, second row*) in a picture parade from his High School Yearbook.

That is about all of Buddy Holly to be found in his home town—a town which prides itself on its strong religious traditions (it is home to several hundred different religious groups, contains dozens of churches and has been described as the 'Buckle of the Bible Belt'), boasts of its 'dry' reputation where the sale of alcohol is concerned, and whose generally friendly citizens enjoy a laid-back attitude to life. Yet, though there are those who claim Lubbock *is* proud of the young man who helped change modern music in a few brief years, whose records became and remain famous around the world, and who is today a legend, the fact is he remains almost without honour in his home town. Certainly not so royally commemorated as Elvis Presley.

But still, the facts of Buddy Holly's early life and his subsequent remarkable achievements in the world of show business are there for the tracing—and any such trail must, inevitably, begin in Lubbock . . .

*   *   *

Buddy was born Charles Hardin Holley on 7 September, 1936, the youngest of the four children of Lawrence and Ella Holley. Mr Holley, an enterprising young man from the north-east of Texas, had moved wherever there was work during the years of the Depression, and it was in 1925 that he settled in the growing town of Lubbock with his new wife. Lawrence Holley found work in the clothing business which had evolved from the booming cotton industry, and there the couple raised their children, Larry (born 1925), Travis (1927), Patricia (1929) and Buddy who arrived at their home on 1911, 6th Street in 1936.

Named after his two grandfathers, the little fellow showed himself rather livelier than the two somewhat austere names which he had been given, and he was soon known as Buddy by the whole family. Though he was never overly spoiled by his parents and elder brothers and sister, Buddy undoubtedly reaped the rewards of the youngest child in a family as a better standard of living replaced their initial straitened circumstances.

The Holley family, with the exception of Mr Holley, apparently enjoyed making music amongst themselves—the elder sons could play the guitar and piano, while Mrs Holley and Patricia enjoyed harmony singing—and with the family's encouragement little Buddy was entered for a local talent content at the tender age of five. Here he won a special prize singing 'Down The River of Memories', accompanying himself on a toy violin!

Until he was eleven years old, however, Buddy showed no particular inclination to play a musical instrument. Instead, overcoming the poor eyesight which was later to necessitate the most famous of his trademarks—the black-rimmed spectacles—the youngster enjoyed Little League baseball, swimming and hunting, and for several years was a keen member of the Wolf Cubs. Buddy's Cub Card was printed with the unconsciously humorous line, 'I promise to do my best: 1. To be Square . . .'

An important influence on Buddy's life through these formative years was the local Tabernacle Baptist Church to which the family belonged and attended regularly. (This branch of the Baptists is classified as Fundamentalist, believing in the literal truth of the Bible.) And though there is no suggestion that little Buddy sprang from his seat during a service and broke into song as Elvis Presley is said to have done, thereby revealing his natural talent to all the world, it is true that the hymns sung in this particular church were closer to popular music than traditional religious music.

"The Raven"
By Edgar Allen Poe

Once upon a midnight dreary, while I pondered,
            weak and weary,
Over many a quaint and curious volume of
            forgotten lore,
While I nodded, nearly napping, suddenly there
            came a tapping,
As of someone gently rapping, rapping at my
            chamber door,
'Tis the wind and nothing more.

Ah, distinctly I remember, It was in the bleak
            December,
And each separate, dying ember wrought its
            ghost upon the floor.
Eagerly, I wished the morrow, vainly I had sought
            to borrow,
From my books surcease of sorrow, sorrow for
            the lost Lenore,

One of Buddy Holly's earliest influences was the tragic American poet, Edgar Allan Poe—and Buddy copied out the lines of one of his famous poems, 'The Raven'.

The Minister of the Tabernacle Church during Buddy's teenage years and early fame was the Reverend Ben Johnson, and an illuminating story is told in Lubbock about a service at which the Minister delivered a thundering attack on rock 'n' roll as being 'sent by the Devil to corrupt the young'.

Seated listening to this sermon were Buddy and the two other members of The Crickets, who squirmed uncomfortably as the rest of the congregation chorused their approval at the sentiments. At the end of his sermon, the Reverend Mr Johnson announced that the collection that week was for a new church window, for which the appeal fund was still $25,000 short.

The story goes that when the plate reached Buddy he took out his chequebook and wrote a cheque for the entire amount. The following week the preacher was still decrying the evils of rock 'n' roll—'but he wasn't yelling quite so loud!'

Another influence on young Buddy Holly was the poetry of the tortured American genius, Edgar Allan Poe (1809–1849), whose writings were part of the English syllabus at both Hutchinson Junior High and Lubbock High School. Surviving school work books show that during his junior school years Buddy wrote a perceptive essay on the 'great romanticist of doom', and that at the High School he copied out Poe's famous poem 'The Raven' as part of a project. There is a great deal of unrequited love to be found in Poe's poems, and there are lines in some of Buddy's songs which betray a debt to the poet.

Despite a claim that was made on some of Buddy's early records that his interest in music began at the age of eight through playing the violin, according to his mother, Ella, it was not until her son was about eleven that she thought he should learn a musical instrument like his brothers, and paid for him to have piano tuition with one of his school teachers. Although he did not continue these lessons for very long, the youngster displayed a natural aptitude for the piano, and even when the guitar had become his favourite instrument he still enjoyed sitting down at the keyboard whenever the opportunity arose and playing to amuse himself or his friends.

It was in the autumn of 1949 that Buddy asked his parents for a guitar and was given one of the standard acoustic guitars so popular at that time with American youngsters. He was now the proud owner of the instrument of his destiny.

Although Bill Griggs maintains that Buddy was poor at school—'a complete nerd' is his actual description—and the boy himself admitted that he was not much of a student, a copy of the 1949 Lubbock High School Yearbook which has survived in the local library reveals that he was given the title 'King of Grade School' that year—though quite what accomplishments had earned him this accolade is hard to discover! And although it is evident that he only played the guitar for his own pleasure at this time, Buddy did develop his ability as a singer by joining The Choralaires at the High School in 1953. The school yearbook for that year shows Buddy singing in the choir, and also in its pages are photographs of classmate Bob Montgomery, shortly to become his first musical partner, as well as Jerry Allison and Niki Sullivan, two other local boys who would later become members of The Crickets. Pictured, too, is the prettily-named Echo McGuire, Buddy's first girlfriend.

It was Bob Montgomery, a round-faced, tousled-haired boy, with a passion for Country and Western music, who turned Buddy's casual interest in the guitar into something more specific. Bob was not only keen on playing guitar but also loved listening to the various local radio stations which could be picked up in Lubbock—in particular the Grand Ole Opry from WSM Nashville and the

Louisiana Hayride from KWKH Shreveport. He and Buddy were soon firm friends, rarely apart, and often to be found practising their guitars together.

It is generally agreed that the most profound early influence on Buddy Holly was the ill-fated singer Hank Williams. Born on a farm in Georgiana, Alabama, in September 1923, he, like Buddy a Virgo, was also given a guitar as a present by his parents and won a talent contest while still a young shaver. A star by 1949 both for his songwriting and his records, Williams gave the music world such all-time classics as 'Your Cheating Heart' and 'Cold, Cold Heart', and was dead of alcohol and drugs by January 1953, aged just 29.

The unforgettable sound of Hank Williams' voice, his heartrending lyrics —'Lovesick Blues' was one of Buddy's favourite songs—and the tragic but romantic story of his life as something of a loner and a musical rebel, appealed to the two boys who learned to play along with his records with almost faultless precision.

Another great influence on Buddy was the Country & Western singer, Hank Williams, who also died tragically young . . .

There is evidence that Buddy and Bob first demonstrated their talents for other classmates at Lubbock High School, graduating from these impromptu sessions to actual school functions such as assemblies and parents' evenings. It is believed they first appeared in public at the Hi-D-Ho drive-in, a restaurant the two had regularly visited with other friends. A local story claims Buddy Holly actually made his first public appearance on the roof of this restaurant!

A handwritten 'contract' that recently came to light certainly establishes that Buddy was playing publicly in May 1954. The document, in Buddy's own hand, is drawn up between Brownfield High School in Brownfield, Texas, and a group calling themselves The Rhythm Playboys, to play at a dance in the school on the evening of 4 May in return for 'fifty percent (50%) of all receipts collected from the stage'. Those named as the members of the group are Buddy and Bob, plus two other friends, David Bowen and Jack Neal.

As well as such evidence of early business acumen, Buddy also signed himself up as member number four of 'The Club For Unappreciated Musicians', founded by one Tommy Hancock. Buddy wrote above the space for type of instrument the single word, 'vocal'.

Buddy's membership card to 'The Club for Unappreciated Musicians'.

There is a bizarre little story about this membership card. For years Buddy carried it around, with his driving licence, club cards and money, in a black leather wallet which he lost while water ski-ing at Buffalo Lakes, Lubbock, in August 1958, six months before his death. Only a matter of days after the plane crash in Iowa, the lake was being cleaned and the wallet suddenly reappeared. The contents inside were remarkably still intact—though very damp—and as a

Echo McGuire

God bless you as you graduate --
And may He grant to you
His love, His help, and guidance
In the things you plan and do.

Forever a memory
Echo

MAY 27 '55

result were returned to the Holley family. As a further twist to this story, also folded in the wallet was an air travel card . . .

Buddy could be high spirited, too, and was not above a bit of mischief —particularly when borrowing the family car. He was issued with his first driver's licence in 1953, aged 16, and within the next couple of years was several times caught for speeding, as well as other traffic violations including driving without a licence and driving without a muffler (exhaust). Perhaps not surprisingly, he lost his licence for six months!

Though there are reports of Buddy at this period of his life which describe him as a 'skinny, freckle-faced brat', he was not unpopular with girls and enjoyed a close relationship with pretty Echo McGuire who inscribed a Christmas card to him in 1954: 'To my SWEETHEART at Christmas—with lots of love, Echo'. (In 1955, Echo left Lubbock to go to college and the couple's paths never crossed again.) He was not lacking in self-confidence, either, for also among his school papers were found a self-portrait of himself wearing a badge, 'I Like Me', and a notebook in which he had written pen portraits of his friends, the first page bearing the words: 'Buddy Holly—Love Him, keen guy, handsome, conceited?'

As far as his parents were concerned, Buddy appeared to have no real idea of a career as his schooldays drew to a close, although to ease their anxieties about his future he had enrolled in special classes for printing and draughtsmanship and joined the 'Vocational Industrial Club of Co-operative Training' of which he was made a Vice-President. But in a school essay, 'My Autobiography', written in 1953, his thoughts were obviously beginning to move in another, quite different direction.

'I have many hobbies,' he wrote. 'Some of these are hunting, fishing, leather-work, reading, painting and playing western music. I have thought about making a career out of western music if I am good enough, but I will just have to wait to see how that turns out.'

Events were about to conspire to make that decision arrive rather sooner for Buddy Holly than he had expected . . .

VIC of ICT Attends District Convention

Nineteen different trades are engaged in by the 36 members of Vocational Industrial Club of Industrial Co-operative Training, Chapter 95. These students work afternoons and have a business meeting once a week.

Socials included a formal initiation at K. N. Clapp Party House and an Employer-Employee Banquet. Tuesday nights the group played basketball or volleyball in the boys' gym.

Representatives went to a district meet in Amarillo and the state meet at Waco. Lawana Hilburn attended these as club sweetheart.

Officers are, clockwise, Charlene Hada-way, secretary; Buddy Holly, vice-president; and Delton Combs, president. Not pictured are James Hogan, treasurer; Bob Montgomery, reporter; and Don Adams, sergeant-at-arms.

Members are Delton Combs, Buddy Holly, Charlene Hadaway, James Hogan, Bob Montgomery, Don Adams, Sarah Adams, J. C. Alexander, Don Allen, David Bowers, Carolyn Cone, Lawrence Dale, Aubrey Davis, James Fread, Reagan Garrett, Eugene Green, Billy Henson, Lawana Hilburn, Amos Hodge, Henry Housour, George Jones, John Jackson, Wayne Jacobs, Don Ledwig, Bobby Mayfield, Jimmie Oglesby, Beverly Patrick, John A. Petty, James Pritchard, Mary Robertson, Norman Williamson, Frank Wilson, Herbert Wilson, Harold Womack, Eddie Yuzbick, and Ray Nall.

Opposite: A rare photograph of Buddy with his girlfriend, Echo McGuire, and a graduation card which she sent him. Above: Buddy the businessman-to-be? Vice-President Buddy Holly of the 'Vocational Industrial Club of Co-operative Training'. Note that Buddy's first musical partner, Bob Montgomery, is listed as the group's 'reporter'!

SEE! HEAR!
IN PERSON
ELVIS
PRESLEY
TONIGHT
FRIDAY—7:00 AT
JOHNSON-CONNELLEY
PONTIAC SHOW ROOM
AT MAIN AND
(No Admission Charge)

Good Rockin' Tonight!

The evening of Friday, 6 April, 1955 was like the start of most weekends for the people of Lubbock: a night to stay at home, relax over a quiet meal after a hard week's work, and perhaps listen to the radio. All of them, that is, except for those young people who loved live music, because a group of country artists—including an up-and-coming young singer called 'The Hillbilly Cat' who some people were already saying was going to be a big star—was appearing at the Cotton Club.

This club, a sprawling barn of a place, was the town's leading country music dance hall and a mecca for fans of C & W. The local country music radio station, KDAV, was responsible for putting on regular shows at the club, and the station's founder and energetic disc jockey, Dave 'Pappy' Stone, organised the line-up of talent.

The biggest attractions at these shows were invariably the artists who had appeared on the Grand Ole Opry in Nashville or on the Louisiana Hayride in Shreveport, because their records were familiar to the local fans. Among the most popular in Lubbock were Slim Whitman, Faron Young, The Carter Sisters (one of whom would later marry singer Johnny Cash) and the multi-talented Ferlin Huskey, who sometimes doubled as comedian-singer 'Simon Crum'.

Obviously it was not possible for Dave Stone to book in headliners every week at the Cotton Club, and on this night in April, the artists included a singing duo, J.E. and Maxine Brown, a warbling cowboy singer called Onie Wheeler, and 'The Hillbilly Cat', a certain Elvis Presley, with his two musicians, Scotty Moore and Bill Black.

Ever since July the previous year, with the release of his first record on the Sun

Opposite: Elvis Presley, the 'Hillbilly Cat', who brought rock 'n' roll to Lubbock—and caught the imagination of Buddy Holly. The Gibson acoustic Elvis is playing in the centre picture is the one Buddy copied when he added his initials in leather to his own guitar. Below is a rare photograph of Elvis outside the Cotton Club in Lubbock. Circled, right, are young fans Buddy Holly and Bob Montgomery. At the top of the page, the advertisement for Elvis' performance at the Johnson-Connelley Car Show Rooms, at which Buddy also appeared.

label, 'That's All Right, Mama', the reputation of this young singer with the negro-sounding voice and gyrating stage performance had been growing throughout the South. For despite the legends which claim Elvis achieved 'overnight success', he actually spent two years developing his style—and it is also true that his debut disc, 'That's All Right, Mama', only sold 20,000 copies, far fewer than the cover version by the country music star, Marty Robbins.

Among the teenagers who filed into the Cotton Club that night were Buddy Holly and Bob Montgomery, who had both heard Presley on the radio and were hoping to pick up some tips for their own act. For Buddy it had been Elvis' quintessential invitation to rock, 'Good Rockin' Tonight'—his second Sun release, which he had sung all over the South in dance hall auditoriums in the months following its release the previous September—that had really captivated him. If any one song could be said to have fired his enthusiasm for rock, it was this one. And the night he first heard it sung in person was to have a profound effect on the rest of his career. It was also to mark the beginning of a number of interesting parallels in the lives of both the singer and his admirer.

Dave Stone, who had been responsible for booking Presley into Lubbock and later watched the rise to fame of Buddy Holly, has a special place in local music history as well as in country music in general. After a number of years as a DJ on another Lubbock station, KSEL, he had decided to open a new station of his own on the outskirts of the town, devoted entirely to country music. And in September 1953 KDAV had gone on the air with Dave and two other men who shared his musical tastes, Hi Pockets Duncan and Ben Hall.

Dave, who now lives in Colorado Springs and runs one of several music stations he still owns, has never forgotten his years in Lubbock and the young singer whose career he first saw develop.

'I always loved country music,' he says in his still unmistakable Texan drawl. 'Hank Williams was my idol. I'd been around radio for years before I got a licence to run KDAV. The call sign was based on my name, and I'm proud of the fact that it was the first full-time country music station to open in America.'

Buddy's tribute to Elvis (*right*) which he made in September 1958, and (*left*) Dave Stone, the Lubbock disc jockey and radio station owner who gave Buddy Holly his first break.

Buddy and Bob Montgomery modelled their early style of performing as 'The Buddy and Bob Show' on the popular Bluegrass country singers, Lester Flatt and Earl Scraggs, seen here on the 'Grand Ole Opry'.

'I figure it was in the fall of 1953, round about Christmas time, when I first heard Buddy Holly. He was still at high school then. On Sunday afternoons we ran this show, "Sunday Party", where we booked country stars as headliners and also ran a talent contest. A lot of the people who came on the show were older folk, but sometimes we got teenagers like Buddy and his friend, Bob Montgomery. The very first show they appeared on it was plain obvious that Buddy had talent.

'My partner Hi Pockets Duncan offered the boys a regular spot on "Sunday Party" and they got themselves a bass player [another Lubbock schoolfriend, Larry Welborn]. They called themselves "The Buddy and Bob Show", after Lester Flatt and Earl Scruggs, a pair of Bluegrass country singers who were very big on the Louisiana Hayride around that time. In fact, they played a lot of Flatt and Scruggs numbers on the show. Funny thing, at that time Buddy Holly didn't do as much of the singing as his partner, he just stood and picked on his guitar!'

Another picker who caught Dave's attention in the summer of 1954 was Elvis Presley, and Dave and Hi Pockets were among the first DJs outside Elvis' home town, Memphis, to air his records.

'When Elvis first got started he was considered country,' Dave continues. 'Sure he had a new kinda sound that the kids liked, but most DJs just mixed his records in with all the other Country and Western artists. We played his singles on KDAV and after a bit called them rockabilly. [See the article 'Rockabilly' (opposite) for a contemporary account of this phenomenom from *Billboard Magazine*, November 1963.]

'We thought of rockabilly as just another kind of country music, so we always played it. Elvis was billed right alongside the other country stars like Ferlin Huskey and Marty Robbins and I know I did well with it. I bought some other stations in the area and the sizes of their audiences kept going up. Mind you, in them early days Elvis only got paid $35 for a show—and he had to split the take with Scotty Moore and Bill Black!

'Of course, that was all before he started creating riots and people began attacking him in churches and in the newspapers. But I thought he was a real polite boy and we certainly didn't have any trouble with him at the Cotton Club.'

A rare photograph—reproduced in this book—of Elvis after his performance in Lubbock in April 1955, graphically supports Dave's story and shows him amongst an orderly crowd of youngsters outside the Cotton Club. And there, on the far right of the picture, are Buddy and Bob hoping for a closer look at 'The Hillbilly Cat' whose performance had so impressed them.

It was not until Elvis paid a second visit to Lubbock in June, however, that the two local boys plucked up the courage to speak to the young rocker. By then they, too, were a part of the show rather than members of its audience.

Elvis returned on Friday, 3 June, this time as part of an all-star package in which he was still only a featured performer rather than the star. The headliner was Ferlin Huskey, with Martha Carson, The Carlisles, J.E. and Maxine Brown, Onie Wheeler and Elvis. The group had already played across Texas from Fort Worth to Dallas, Abilene, Midland, Odessa and Amarillo before reaching Lubbock.

For the show that night, Buddy with Bob and Larry were the opening act, followed by Elvis—a clear indication of 'The Hillbilly Cat's' status in the pecking order! And according to contemporary reports, at the end of the show it was Ferlin Huskey who had to climb out of his dressing room window to avoid a horde of autograph hunters, while Elvis walked out of the Cotton Club quite unmolested.

Earlier—bolder now because he was a performer in the show—Buddy introduced himself to Elvis backstage. The singer from Memphis was sitting on his own having a soft drink and didn't mind in the least when Buddy came over and spoke to him.

The musicians soon found they shared a common interest in rhythm and blues music, and Buddy told Elvis that he and his partner were hoping to make some records themselves. They had already made a trip to a small recording facility, the Nesman Studios in Wichita Falls, to make a demonstration tape of some songs, and had then tried unsuccessfully to interest a local representative of Columbia Records. (These songs were all written by Bob and strongly C & W in style.)

Elvis listened politely to Buddy's story, offered what encouragement he could, and left the Lubbock teenager very pleased at the interest he had shown.

"*ROCKABILLY*"

a fusion of Country and Rock 'N' Roll

One of the most important musical trends in the history of pop music has been the so-called "rockabilly" influence. The term is descriptive and accurate, for this type of performance represents a fusion of both rock and roll and country (or, to use an older slang term, hillbilly) elements.

The key catalyst in this development —which occurred during the past decade—has been Sam Phillips, head of Sun Records of Memphis. Phillips is known throughout the record world as the man who found Elvis Presley, often termed "the greatest rocker of them all."

This piece of talent scouting alone would assure Phillips a niche in the annals of the record business. But his subsequent talent finds indicated the Presley acquisition was no mere flash in the pan. In succession, Phillips acquired and scored big hits with Carl Perkins, Johnny Cash, Jerry Lee Lewis, Roy Orbison and, more recently, Charlie Rich. In short, Phillips struck a remarkably rich vein of talent, most of which subsequently went on to other labels and thereby facilitated the expansion of the rockabilly influence.

"Rockabilly" connotes both a type of material and a style of performance. As to the former, it is interesting to note that much of the material is blues-based. Sam Phillips had a profound grounding in the blues idiom. In the early years of his career he became interested in this vital area of American music and recorded primitive country blues and urban blues with such artists as Muddy Waters and Jackie Brenston, B. B. King, Howlin' Wolf, Roscoe Gordon and others.

In experimenting with the blues idiom, Phillips ultimately began to seek artists who could give this musical form a new sound—in brief, white artists who dug both country and blues material. The fact that country artists understand blues is widely known — and discerning observers have often pointed out that there has always been a strong blues tradition in the country field.

As to the type of performance, the rockabilly style emphasized a robust vocal performance backed with guitar instrumentation in an arrangement notable for solid rhythm. The early Presley recordings on the Sun label— such as "Mystery Train" and many of his later sides on RCA Victor, such as "I Gotta Woman," illustrate this point.

It is to be noted parenthetically, of course, that RCA Victor broadened Presley's appeal—both with regard to style of performance and use of song material. He ultimately scored in all aspects of pop music, but his initial sides were models of what came to be known as rockabilly.

The music trade—as well as students of American music—have often speculated as to whether the Presley records, or rockabilly, could be properly included in the category of country music. Presley, and many of the other noted artists who started on the Sun label, did not develop through the usual country music channels.

Is He Real?

Presley, for instance, achieved wide fame without maturing over the noted country music program, WSM's "Grand Ole Opry." And it is accurate and fair to state that fans of the traditional country school protested Presley's appearance on the best selling country record charts. "He is not real country," was a common remark. Others, however, took a broader view, pointing out that country music included the blues tradition. Those harboring this view proudly claimed Presley and other great rockabillies as part and parcel of the country field. Thus, there are these two points of view.

In any event, the contribution of Phillips, Presley and others to the over-all music scene cannot be minimized; for Presley alone, it is estimated, has sold approximately $75,-000,000 worth of records; and Phillips through the rockabilly channel added a distinctive element and sound to pop music.

'You know,' Buddy was quoted as saying later, 'Elvis is a real nice friendly fellow.'

The two met up again when Elvis was booked to sing at the opening of the new Johnson-Connelley Pontiac Car Show Room in Lubbock. ('No Admission Charge', an advertisement in the *Lubbock Evening Journal* declared!) Buddy and his trio followed Elvis this time, and played several numbers to the crowds who gathered in the showroom to look at the rows of new automobiles. On Saturday, Buddy took Elvis on a tour of Lubbock before the singer moved on with the other touring artists.

There is no doubt that Buddy was very impressed by Elvis both as a performer and a man. As Presley historian Terry Mailey has written, 'Buddy was so impressed with Elvis' leather-bound guitar that he made a similar cover for his own Gibson. Elvis' stage wear also impressed Buddy and he began wearing loud stage clothes—red jackets and bright red shoes with white trousers appealed to him. Buddy clearly idolised Elvis and he thereafter included at least one of his numbers in every set he played.'

Another important influence attributed to Elvis was Buddy's decision to recruit a drummer for his group after Elvis had added D. J. Fontana to his combo. Schoolfriend Jerry Allison, who had been practising hard on his drumming, was the man chosen to fill this spot. It has been suggested, too, that Buddy Holly seriously thought about going to Elvis' recording label, Sun, to try and get an audition—but a rumour that he actually *did* cut some demonstration sides for Sam Phillips' innovative label is without any foundation.

Elvis' parting words to his new friend as he left Lubbock this time was that he should try and get on the Louisiana Hayride in Shreveport. 'The Hillbilly Cat' said he believed the show to be an important stepping stone in any local artist's career. If Buddy did decide to go, Elvis added, he would use what influence he had to get him on the show. The words rang like music in Buddy Holly's ears . . .

When, however, a few weeks later, Buddy, Bob and Larry had saved enough money to make the long journey to Shreveport, they were met only by disappointment. Though the trio boldly informed the Hayride producer, Horace Logan, that Elvis had suggested they audition for the show, they were curtly told that the rock 'n' roller was away on tour and were shown the door!

Though it is true the paths of Buddy and Elvis Presley never crossed again, the parallels in their subsequent lives are quite remarkable. Just as Elvis began his career with a record especially for his mother, 'That's All Right, Mama', so one of Buddy's earliest numbers was 'Have You Ever Been Lonely?' a long-time favourite of Mrs Holley. Like Elvis, Buddy was turned down by the Grand Ole Opry in Nashville, and he, too, made his television debut on the Ed Sullivan Show from New York.

And, later, with some of his earnings from success, Buddy copied Elvis by buying himself a powerful motorcycle (an Ariel Cyclone) and set his ultimate career target of becoming a major movie star. In the late 'Fifties, the two men were frequently mentioned in the same breath by the Press and a famous front-page story from the *Lubbock Evening Journal* of 23 October, 1956 declares in its headlines: 'BUDDY HOLLY PACKS 'EM IN—YOUNG SINGER IS LUBBOCK'S ANSWER TO ELVIS PRESLEY'. Buddy, of course, recorded some of Elvis' songs—notably 'Baby, Let's Play House' which he called 'I Wanna Play House With You', and 'Baby, I Don't Care', again retitled 'You're So Square'—and this compliment was returned by Elvis after Buddy's death.

Both men, of course, suffered tragic deaths, and since then have been the subject of curious rumours that they are still alive! In Buddy's case, the sighting of UFOs—Flying Saucers—over Lubbock has been taken by the more credulous as a sign that he might have been of extraterrestrial origin!

Elvis Presley was not, however, the only pioneer of rock 'n' roll with whom Buddy Holly appeared in 1955. In October of that same year, Bill Haley and the Comets made a special appearance at the Fair Park Coliseum in Lubbock. That show on 14 October is generally regarded as the one in which Buddy got his break into show business.

Haley, born in Highland Park, Michigan, in 1925, had struggled to success from an impoverished childhood by learning guitar and raising a band of country musicians (initially called The Saddlemen) who worked long and hard for recognition. Short-sighted (like Buddy) and sporting a kiss-curl, Bill Haley was another unlikely-looking star, but his unique style of rockabilly, which he had been developing ever since his first single, 'Rock This Joint', was released in 1951, grabbed the nation's youth and made him internationally famous. By 1954 he

Bill Haley, here with members of his group, The Comets, used Buddy as a backing musician when he appeared in Lubbock in 1955—and by so doing gave the youngster another push along the road to fame.

was being referred to in the Press as 'the king of rock 'n' roll', riding high on the success of his recording, 'Rock Around The Clock', which in 1955 became the theme song of the controversial movie about teenage violence, *Blackboard Jungle*. The movie had been released only a few months before Haley and the Comets came to Lubbock.

Bill Haley and Buddy were destined to appear on the same bill a number of times and become friends, although their initial meeting certainly had an element of farce about it. But out of a somewhat unlikely situation, Buddy was to find himself on the road to a recording contract.

In 1981—the year before his own death—Bill Haley talked about his memories of Buddy and their first meeting.

'He was a very sociable kid, very friendly,' the rock veteran said. 'He liked to spend time with other musicians in their dressing rooms before concerts and afterwards, talking about music and listening to songs. I am sure he would have had a long and successful career if he had lived.

'I remember our first meeting in Lubbock very clearly. The boys and I were doing a one-night stand in the local stadium and Buddy had just got started. We drove to Lubbock in two cars, and on the way there the other car with the boys in got a flat tyre. My manager and I were in the lead car and we decided to go on and leave them to get the tyre fixed.

'When we got to the stadium, the place was full and there was pandemonium. We told the promoter what had happened and said we hoped the boys would be along shortly. After a while he came back and said I would have to go on or there would be a riot. I said, "How can I go on with no band and no instruments?"

'So he told me he had these kids who would go on with me. And he introduced Buddy Holly. This was before he had made any records or anything. Anyhow, we all went out onto the stage and we did probably half an hour before my band got there. Buddy was very good and you could tell even then that he was going to be a star. I read later that this agent Eddie Crandall saw Buddy that night and offered to try and get him a recording contract in Nashville.'

It was to be a couple of years later before Bill Haley met his erstwhile co-star again. By then, Buddy was a recording star in his own right and the two men came face to face in the Decca Record Offices in New York. A few months afterwards they were reunited on the stage when Buddy shared the limelight with Bill and the wild man of rock, Jerry Lee Lewis, for three days of concerts in Jacksonville, Florida.

They were scheduled to meet once more, but fate intervened. Bill Haley's voice dropped as he recalled this finale to their friendship.

'We were on this one-night tour in January-February 1959,' he said. 'I forget just where we were the night Buddy was killed. But we were due to appear with him the next night. We didn't know what had happened until we got to Moorhead. I had hoped to see him again, but of course I didn't. We all lost a great talent that day.'

But tragedy was still a long way off the night when Buddy played backing man to Bill Haley—although his first experience of recording, which lay just over the horizon in Nashville, Tennessee, was to prove far from the success the young singer had been dreaming about . . .

Don't Come
Back Knocking

Nashville, which stands beside the Cumberland River in the heart of Tennessee not far from the Appalachian Mountains, has been called the 'Athens of the South', but to pop record lovers everywhere it is better known as 'Music City, USA'. Although it rose to fame as the home of country music, its large number of studios and superb recording facilities have made it a popular spot with artists from all over the world who come to make single releases as well as albums.

Elvis Presley, for one, cut many of his finest records in Nashville—including 'Heartbreak Hotel', the most famous of all his hits, which made him a world-wide celebrity in 1956—and apart from other great American artists like Dylan, Paul Simon and Roy Orbison, top stars from Britain and Europe have also made the long trek to add the unique 'Nashville Sound' to their songs. Notable among British stars have been Elvis Costello who bears a striking physical resemblance to Buddy Holly and likewise wears glasses with thick black rims!

Although it was Sam Phillips in his little studio in Memphis, who had been mainly instrumental in creating the rock 'n' roll revolution in 1954, Nashville still remained the mecca to which most new artists migrated. There they hoped to find a label which would record them as well as perhaps get a chance to appear on the weekly 'Grand Ole Opry', a showcase of talent which in the 'Fifties was almost a guaranteed passport to fame.

The Ryman Auditorium in downtown Nashville, in which the 'Grand Ole Opry' was staged, was built in 1891 by a roistering river boat captain, Tom Ryman, who 'found' religion and had the building constructed as somewhere for revivalist meetings to be held. In 1925 its purpose was changed to provide home-spun entertainment, and soon sacred songs were mingling with country

music to raise the rafters. And when the Saturday night shows began to be broadcast over WSM radio, followed by television transmissions, both of which reached ever-increasing audiences throughout the South, the Opry's reputation and those who sang and played on its enormous stage grew phenomenally.

Among those artists whose careers were made at the Opry can be listed Hank Williams (whose 'Cold, Cold Heart' was perhaps the first country song to 'cross over' into pop music), followed by Marty Robbins, Hank Snow, Red Foley, Ernest Tubb, Jim Reeves, Faron Young, Ferlin Husky, Chet Atkins, Patsy Cline, Brenda Lee, Johnny Cash and the Everly Brothers. Although, as mentioned earlier, Elvis Presley failed to make an impact on the Opry audience, his backing-group, The Jordanaires, were regulars on the show.

But for every artist who succeeded on the Opry—or in one of the dozens of recording studios in the city which drew stars from its auditorium and provided it with talented newcomers—hundreds, even thousands, of other young men and women, white and black, went away disappointed and disillusioned. Visitors to Nashville in the middle and late 1950s, of whom I was one, were constantly amazed at the number of musicians and singers to be found on street corners trying to earn some small change to keep themselves alive while they searched for a break in 'Music City'.

Buddy Holly was therefore understandably a little apprehensive when he made the four-hundred-mile drive from Lubbock to Nashville for his first recording session on 26 January, 1956. Interestingly, he was travelling much the same route as Elvis who, on 10 January, as a result of his contract with Sun Records being taken over by the mighty RCA label (thanks to the shrewd negotiations of his new manager, Colonel Tom Parker), had gone to the company's studios at 1525, McGavock Street to cut several numbers, including 'Heartbreak Hotel'. The major difference, however, was that Elvis' style had been appreciated for what it was by the RCA boss in Nashville, Steve Sholes, whereas Buddy was being considered in much more traditional country style by his potential label, Decca.

Opposite: Nashville—'Music City'—the musical mecca in which Buddy found only frustration and disappointment. Left: The Ryman Auditorium in Nashville, home of the 'Grand Ole Opry' (*below*) which Buddy visited in November 1956 with dreams of stardom.

The man who had been responsible for setting up this recording session was Eddie Crandall, the manager of country star Marty Robbins, who had appeared in Lubbock at the end of October on another Cotton Club bill organised by Dave Stone, which had also featured Buddy and Bob.

Marty Robbins, a genial and versatile singer born in Glendale, Arizona, in 1925, took to singing on radio shows in the South after his discharge from the Navy in 1946, and was a star of the Grand Ole Opry from 1953 onwards; he found his path crossing that of Buddy Holly several times during the young Texan's short life.

'Buddy Holly appeared with me in Lubbock in the winter of 1955,' Marty recalled a few years ago. 'He was a skinny kid, but had these amazing guitar hands. He had a real feel for the instrument.

'He was also a really determined guy. He said he was going to write his own songs and sing them on record. I have always reckoned that songwriters and guitar players are born and not made, and that sure applied to Buddy Holly. He just had this inborn talent.

'He was always ready to play for anyone who would listen. I remember that he and his group opened the show at the Cotton Club and when it was over we all sat around in my dressing room shooting the breeze. After a while Buddy picked up his guitar and started a jam session that just went on and on until the early hours. Buddy had such energy, you just couldn't keep him down. If he wasn't playing he was talking about what he wanted to do. And his biggest ambition was to make a record.'

In Lubbock with Marty Robbins that night was his manager, Eddie Crandall. 'I told Eddie that I thought Buddy had what it takes to become a star, so why didn't he try and get the boy a recording contract? Eddie had a lot of contacts in Nashville and I figured if anyone could open a door for the boy it would be him.'

One of the first people Eddie Crandall spoke to about Buddy was, apparently, Elvis' new manager, Tom Parker. The 'Ole Colonel' was not surprisingly up to his eyes in work promoting his new signing and couldn't help. However, through another friend, Jim Denny, a booking agent for the 'Grand Ole Opry', Crandall did get an introduction to Decca, one of the major country labels based in Nashville, and two of its senior men, the head of country music, Paul Cohen, and his chief a. & r. man, Owen Bradley.

Eddie talked enthusiastically about Buddy to the two Decca men and got their agreement to listen to some demonstration tracks if the artist sent them up to Nashville. A telegram from Crandall to Buddy in Lubbock via Dave Stone urged: 'HAVE BUDDY HOLLY CUT 4 ORIGINAL SONGS ON ACETATE. DON'T CHANGE HIS STYLE AT ALL. GET THESE TO ME AS SOON AS POSSIBLE AIR MAIL SPECIAL.'

Buddy set to work eagerly with Bob and Larry, further excited by the fact that Decca was his friend Bill Haley's label. However, when Cohen and Bradley listened to the demos the word went back to Buddy that though Decca were interested in him there was a proviso. They only wanted *him*—there would be no place for Bob Montgomery on the session.

Buddy undoubtedly agonised over what he should do. It was the opportunity he so badly wanted to make a record. But would the price of making it be the loss of his best friend? He decided to play fair with Bob and tell him everything.

Far from being upset, Bob urged his friend to take the chance. Montgomery felt he was more a country singer at heart than a musician in the rockabilly style Buddy wanted to follow. Larry Welborn, younger than the other two and still at

39

Opposite: Marty Robbins, the Nashville Country & Western singer who befriended Buddy Holly in the unwelcoming city.

school, could also not be considered because the recording session was scheduled during term time. Though none of the trio knew it at the time, this was to mark the end of 'The Buddy & Bob Show'.

So with this situation painlessly resolved, Buddy turned to two more of his young Lubbock friends, Sonny Curtis, a guitarist, and a double bass player, Don Guess, to accompany him. The trio drove to Nashville in the Holley family car with Don Guess's bass strapped precariously on the roof. The boys, who confessed later that they must have looked like a bunch of hick musicians, were met at Decca's studios at Bradley's Barn by a quite plainly unimpressed Paul Cohen and Owen Bradley.

Though Cohen and Bradley are important figures in the story of Nashville and country music, they were to do little for Buddy beyond making his first records.

Decca Records in Nashville, which had first opened its doors in 1934 under the aegis of the Decca Company of England, had over the years built up an impressive catalogue of country music. By a curious twist of fate one of the first big stars the label discovered was a dance band group called Milton Brown and the Brownies, whose fame was tragically cut short when the leader died in an automobile accident. Fortunately the company had some 48 tunes on record and were able to satisfy the public demand for Milton Brown discs for many years after his death—a course they were also to follow with Buddy.

In 1945, Paul Cohen had been transferred from Decca's office in Cincinnati and took the label into its golden years of country music. Among his discoveries were Ernest Tubb, Red Foley, and three of C & W's greatest female singers—all of whom made considerable impact on the pop music scene—Kitty Wells, 'The Queen of Country Music', the ill-fated Patsy Cline and, in 1956, 'Little Miss Dynamite', Brenda Lee.

Owen Bradley, a native of Kentucky who masterminded the recording of these artists, was a former piano player who could double as an instrumentalist and an arranger. When he took over the a. & r. position at Decca he already had his own recording studio in Nashville and used this for sessions with many of the label's artists.

It is an interesting and not well-known fact that just prior to working with Buddy Holly, Owen Bradley had a hit record under his own name called 'Blues Stay Away From Me', which had Paul Cohen as musical director and was released on Decca's subsidiary label, Coral. There are those who have listened to this now very rare disc and wondered how the man who made it could ultimately have passed the damning judgement he did on Buddy! Another point worth noting is that in the late 'Fifties Paul Cohen was moved to become head of another label . . . none other than Coral.

Both Cohen and Bradley were dedicated to the traditions of country music, which may help to explain why the ten numbers they cut with Buddy in three sessions during 1956 are so removed from the style by which he will forever be remembered. The details of these sessions are still to be found on file in Decca's offices in Nashville.

On the first of these, on 26 January, Buddy, Sonny and Don were accompanied by two local session men, Grady Martin on rhythm guitar and Buddy Harmon on drums. The songs they recorded were 'Love Me' and the aptly titled (as events transpired) 'Don't Come Back Knocking'—Buddy's first attempts at songwriting and co-written with a Lubbock girl named Sue Parrish. Plus 'Blue Days, Black Nights', penned by Dave Stone's DJ partner at KDAV, Ben Hall, and 'Midnight Days', a number by two unknown writers, Earl Lee and Jimmie Ainsworth, which had just been sent in on spec to Owen Bradley.

There seems little doubt that Buddy's anxiety to please, plus his unmistakable efforts to imitate Elvis, made for a very unsatisfactory first session. Only two tracks, 'Blue Days, Black Nights' and 'Love Me', were issued as a single in April, and made very little impact on the record-buying public. The boys' second visit to Nashville on 22 July was to prove an even bigger let-down.

A new addition to the three musicians for the session was Jerry Allison, who by this time had gained even more valuable experience as a drummer by playing with several bluegrass and jazz groups in the Lubbock area. Jerry and Buddy and the rest spent hours practising together in the Holleys' house before again making the trip to Nashville. In the interim, Buddy had also borrowed the money from his older brother Larry to buy himself a new guitar, the Fender Stratocaster which thereafter became another of his trademarks.

Five tunes were cut on 22 July. The session began with 'Rock Around With Ollie Vee' written by Sonny Curtis; 'Girl On My Mind' by Don Guess; Buddy's Elvis-inspired number 'I'm Changing All Those Changes'; 'Ting-A-Ling', written by the famous Atlantic Records producer, Ahmet Ertegun, and a hit record for the coloured singing group, The Clovers, in 1952; and the first of Buddy's classic numbers, 'That'll Be The Day'.

This last song and its origins in a John Wayne Movie, *The Searchers*, are discussed later in the book; but the fact remains that though Buddy, rightly, was convinced of the tremendous potential of this song, Owen Bradley dismissed it out of hand as 'the worst song I have ever heard'. The session closed under a cloud and it was soon evident to Buddy that Decca were not going to release any of the tracks. (His surmise was quite correct: nothing from the session was pressed until some time after Buddy had rocketed to fame on the Coral label.)

Buddy needed cheering up after this rebuff and found it with Marty Robbins who had an office at 713, 18th Avenue in South Nashville.

'The boys came over to my office and we talked about the sessions,' Marty has recalled. 'Buddy was pretty down because he felt the Decca people didn't understand his style. They were trying to get him to play country when what he wanted to do was play rockabilly. Instead, he ended up making records that were between the two.

'He talked a lot about "That'll Be The Day", he was really keen on that song,' continued Robbins, himself the author of several pop classics like 'Singing The Blues' (which helped make Tommy Steele a household name in Britain), 'White Sport Coat' and the great cowboy refrain 'El Paso'. 'I told him to forget it for the

Opposite: Buddy in the Decca recording studios in Nashville, and the two executives who thought so little of his talent, Paul Cohen (*left*) and Owen Bradley.

BH-49

Although Buddy's experiences with Decca Records in Nashville were largely unhappy, the story that the young singer hit Owen Bradley, as portrayed in the movie, *The Buddy Holly Story*, is apocryphal, though now part of the legend!

time being and go and enjoy himself in Nashville. The place was always full of pretty girls in those days, looking for some action!

'I was also very impressed by this leather cover he had made for his Gibson acoustic guitar. He had coloured the leather black and blue and inscribed the words of his first record, 'Blue Days, Black Nights' and 'Love Me', alongside his own name. I thought it was real smart, and I said if he was short of dollars I would pay him to make some leather wallets for me. He said he would, but they never arrived. I guess success came along in time!'

Buddy recorded his last session for Decca on 15 November—arriving in Nashville while the annual Disc Jockey Festival (still held today) was under way. This time Decca wanted him on his own, and to fill in time, Buddy took in a show at the Grand Ole Opry (dreaming, perhaps, that he might still be up there on the stage one day?) and mingled with disc jockeys from all over the South, who were hustling from one show to the next and one record party to another.

42

But Buddy did not allow himself to be distracted from his purpose of recording, and at the studios learned he was to work with a set of session musicians including Grady Martin on lead guitar and the legendary saxophone player, Boots Randolph. The group of five musicians plus Buddy cut just three tracks: a new version of 'Rock Around With Ollie Vee' and two more Don Guess songs, 'Modern Don Juan' co-written with another Lubbock musician, Jack Neil, and 'You Are My One Desire'. Of these, only 'Modern Don Juan' was to be released at Christmas 1956 and fared just as poorly as 'Blue Days, Black Nights'.

By all accounts the session ended acrimoniously. Buddy was convinced he was not being given a chance to show his real talent, while Paul Cohen was just as obviously convinced he had none. According to one report, Cohen told Buddy he was no singer and should quit the music business. Another story, related by Norman Petty who was later to produce Buddy's hit records, maintains that the Decca chief referred to the young Texan as 'the biggest no-talent I have ever worked with'.

Jerry Allison, the drummer, who had only participated in the July session, shared his friend's sense of frustration and even anger.

'I don't even remember which guy was Paul Cohen and which was Owen Bradley,' he says. 'It was like they were the biggies and we were just dips. We didn't groove with them or anything. We were just sort of afraid of them.'

The situation was not long in being resolved, however. In January 1957, when the option on Buddy's contract came due for renewal, Paul Cohen brusquely informed Eddie Crandall that Decca would not be taking it up. When the news was relayed to Buddy in Lubbock, he felt as if he was right back to square one again. He looked sadly at the pop music charts with Elvis riding high and knew that he and his one-time co-star were now worlds apart.

But how was he ever going to bridge the chasm he so desperately wanted to cross? The sound of a chirping insect was to help provide the unlikely answer . . .

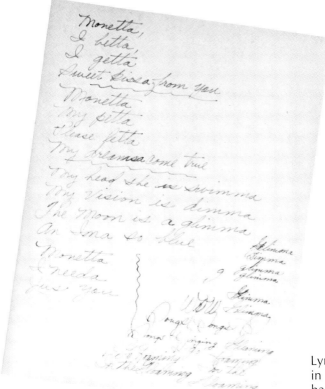

Lyrics of 'Monetta', a song in Buddy's own handwriting, which he composed about this time.

43

That Was the Day!

The state of New Mexico lies in the south-western corner of the United States, sandwiched between the vastness of Texas and the sprawl of Arizona. It is a dry and arid state, beset by dust storms from its red and yellow soils whipped up by winds from towering mountain ranges such as the San Andres and Sacramento Mountains. The state is perhaps best known as the place where the first atomic bomb experiments were carried out, at Los Alamos near the Rio Grande, in July 1945.

Less well known to the public in general is the town of Clovis which lies almost on the crossroads of highways from Lubbock to Albuquerque in the west and Amarillo to Roswell in the south—though in the explosive annals of rock 'n' roll this expanse of low-roofed buildings, just a couple of miles across the border from Texas, has a very special significance. For in an unpretentious and strictly functional two-storey building at 1321, West Seventh Street, two of the giants of modern music cut their first successful records: Roy Orbison and Buddy Holly.

Rather like Buddy's, the fame of Roy Orbison, the man in the dark shades and singer of melodramatic ballads, has grown enormously since his tragically early death of a heart attack at the age of 52 in December 1988. Born in Texas in 1936, Roy was taught to play the guitar by his father, an oil field worker, and by the age of 14 was appearing in his own band, The Wink Westerners. Even in his teens Roy had an extraordinarily powerful voice, heard at its best singing mournful tunes, and a penchant for dressing in black which became his trade mark. Also unprepossessing in appearance, Roy wore thick, black-rimmed glasses and developed a stationary stage performance in contrast to Elvis, Jerry Lee Lewis and the other frantic performers of the 'Fifties. During the latter part of his life, he

Opposite: Joe, Jerry and Buddy with (*inset*) a photograph of Norman Petty's recording studios in Clovis, New Mexico.

earned great sympathy from fans and the general public alike when the personal tragedies behind his songs became known: accidental deaths claimed both his first wife, Claudette, and two of his sons.

On a visit to Britain a few years before his death, Roy talked about the start of his recording career in Clovis and the man who made it all possible, Norman Petty. He also gave his impressions of Buddy Holly.

'I had been playing music around Texas for some years, really getting nowhere,' he said. 'We even changed the band's name from the Wink Westerners to the Teen Kings when Elvis broke the pop mould for all of us. There were a lot of guys like me around then—Buddy Holly also came from my home State of Texas—all writing material and performing any place that would put us on, trying to get a break.

'Then in 1956 I heard about this guy called Norman Petty up in Clovis, New Mexico. They said he was a bit of a wild cat, would let you experiment with new sounds. Looking back today, Norman had the same kind of free approach to music as Sam Phillips at Sun.

'A friend in the business told me Norman was different from most other record producers who charged for studio time by the hour. With him you got to tape a song until you thought it was right. And he had pretty good facilities for someone tucked away in New Mexico.'

Encouraged by what he heard, Roy decided to make the drive to Clovis. He arrived on a scorching hot summer day and had no difficulty finding Petty's studios on the west side with the words 'Nor Va Jak Music' written across the front. The sign incorporated the names of the three partners in the business: Petty himself; his wife, Virginia; and long-time associate Jack Vaughan. The reason for the studio's commendable attitude towards new musicians is not hard to find in Norman Petty's own history, although by his own admission his tastes in the 'Fifties were for easy listening music rather than rockabilly and rock 'n' roll.

Born in Clovis in 1927, he had become fascinated by music as a child, and by the time he had reached his teens was accomplished on several instruments and was also beginning to learn the technical side of music-making through working

Norman Petty, mentor of Buddy Holly and The Crickets.

46

The famous recording sessions in Clovis recreated for the musical, *Buddy*. Buddy (Paul Hipp) discussing his music with Norman Petty (played by Ron Emslie).

at a local radio station. In 1948 he married Vi, a pianist, and recruited Jack Vaughan, a long-time friend and drummer, to form the Norman Petty Trio. Playing 'mood music', the trio worked dates all over the South, and made a number of records which sold well. A version of the Duke Ellington Classic, 'Mood Indigo', in 1954, followed by one of Norman's own compositions called 'Almost Paradise', brought in considerable royalties and the trio decided to invest this in setting up their own commercial recording studio. Apart from being able to make their own records, they also planned to cut discs for other artists and sell them to the major labels with whom Norman had been building up contacts.

Which was precisely what brought Roy Orbison—and, after him, Buddy Holly—to Clovis that summer day.

'Norman was a big, friendly guy with a lovely sense of humour and an easy smile,' said Roy. 'You got the impression right off that he knew a lot about music and recordings and could spot talent, too. Anyhow, I told him I wanted to cut this song I had written called 'Ooby Dooby'. I played him some bars and although I don't believe he dug rock 'n' roll then, he said go right ahead. I made that record and also 'Tryin' To Get To You' for his label Prism Records, but they didn't do much. In fact, it wasn't until I went over to Columbia Records that my career took off.'

For Buddy Holly, this route to success was to be completely reversed—but Roy Orbison remained full of admiration for Norman Petty.

'I learned a lot about the business of making records from Norman,' he said, no doubt thinking of the numerous Top Ten songs he subsequently wrote himself, including 'Claudette', dedicated to his first wife and a smash hit in 1958 for the Everly Brothers, 'Only The Lonely' and 'In Dreams'. 'I guess the same was true of Buddy Holly who went up to Clovis a little after I did. I never actually worked with Buddy, but I love his records and some of the songs he wrote. 'Raining In My Heart' is one of my all-time favourites.'

It was when Buddy Holly realised that his contract with Decca was doomed that he had the idea of contacting Norman Petty, for much the same reasons as Roy Orbison. Clovis was, after all, only a hundred miles from Lubbock and

Buddy's funds had run low with the abortive travelling to and from Nashville. It has lately been suggested that Norman actually knew a bit about the young singer from Lubbock before they met, but his advice when Buddy approached him was terse and to the point.

'I'll make some demos for you,' he said, 'but get yourself a group first and get it together.'

Years later, talking to Chicago journalist Norman Mark about his first impressions of the sharp-featured guitar picker, Petty said, 'When I met him he was wearing a T-shirt and Levis. Really, he was unimpressive to look at, but impressive to hear. In fact, businessmen around Clovis asked me why I was interested in a hillbilly like Holly, and I told them I thought he was a diamond in the rough.

'Buddy was a person ultra-eager to succeed. He knew what he wanted and I knew how to record him. He respected my ability and I respected his personality and talent. He had the eagerness of someone who has something on his mind and wants to do something about it.'

And do something about it is precisely what Buddy Holly did.

Despite the experiences Buddy and Jerry Allison had undergone during the Decca recording session in July 1956, they had continued to play together —sometimes just as a twosome—throughout the autumn and winter. But now they needed at least two more musicians for the demos. A natural choice was Larry Welborn, and after a good deal of trawling the local music scene another guitarist, Niki Sullivan, was added to the line-up. Born in California in 1940, Niki had been moved with his family to Lubbock while still a baby, and with his eyes set on a musical career had financed his playing by working at a number of jobs.

After just over a month of intense practice, the four musicians drove to Clovis on 25 February, 1957, and under Norman Petty's skilful direction cut two songs, both of them written by Buddy: 'I'm Looking For Someone To Love' and a new version of Buddy's old favourite, 'That'll Be The Day'. No sooner had the quartet finished than it became obvious there was one major problem about the second cut. Even though Buddy was no longer contracted to Decca he was still prohibited from recording anything he had made for the label for at least five years.

Norman Petty came up with the solution. The boys should give themselves a new name before letting any record company hear the demo disc.

Legend has several stories to relate as to how Buddy and his friends came up with the name which is now a part of music history. One tale maintains that a cricket got loose in the Nor Va Jak studio while the young men were recording and defied all efforts to locate and remove it. The sound of the insect gently chirping on the finished demo disc provided the name of the group . . . so *that* story has it. Another claims the name originally came from a dog belonging to one of Buddy's relatives, of which he was particularly fond.

The real story, however, is far more prosaic. In the middle 'Fifties it was fashionable among young American groups to give themselves the names of animals and birds—the Panthers and the Flamingos are two which spring to mind—and Buddy and Jerry, in looking for a suitable creature, found themselves in the insect pages of an encyclopaedia, and when their eyes lighted on 'cricket' decided their search was over. Though the ensemble would undergo one more change in personnel, 'The Crickets' as we know them were now in being.

Opposite: A rare photograph of Roy Orbison minus the thick-rimmed glasses which became his trade mark as they were Buddy Holly's . . . Overleaf: 'The Little Fella', Joe B. Mauldin, between his six-foot friends, Jerry and Buddy.

While Norman Petty occupied himself trying to interest recording companies in 'The Crickets', Buddy and the others knew they should play some live dates together to be ready if and when the call came from a prospective label. Once again Larry Welborn had to drop out from these plans—and to take his place Jerry Allison introduced one of his friends, Joe B. Mauldin, who although only 16 years old was already an accomplished double bass player.

Mauldin, also born in Lubbock, had been playing musical instruments since he was six, with the encouragement of his mother. He took up bass playing in 1955 and became part of a group, The Four Teens. He was, though, more than happy at being invited to join The Crickets, for he knew of Buddy's reputation locally and had actually seen him playing on several dates.

One particular occasion—Buddy's appearance at the Johnson-Connelley Pontiac Car Show Room special promotion on the same bill with Elvis Presley —has always remained fresh in his mind.

'I was walking by the show room with my mother,' he recalls, 'and she turned to me and said, "Look, there's Elvis Presley." She knew about him from the papers, but she couldn't have looked at the photographs too well, because it was Buddy she pointed at! After I had explained who he really was, we stopped and listened for a while and I guess that was what got me really interested in music.'

Joe thus became the fourth of The Crickets with Buddy, Jerry and Niki—and because he was several inches shorter than the other three six-footers, became affectionately known as 'The Little Fella'.

But while the four young men were establishing their new group, Norman Petty had not been altogether successful in interesting a label in their talent. Roulette Records liked the two songs but wanted a couple of their own artists to record them; while Mitch Miller of Columbia Records (who had heard the early Buddy and Bob tapes) echoed the comment of his opposite number at Decca, Paul Cohen, by declaring Buddy would never make it.

Then, all of a sudden, in March 1957 Norman made a deal—and in the most unexpected quarter.

Petty sent the demo to Bob Thiele, the a. & r. man at Coral Records in New York. Thiele, a chunky, ebullient man, is said by US reporter Charles Govey to have 'at once realised he had potential hit material on his hands', and not only signed Buddy to a solo contract on his label but put together a group agreement for The Crickets to record on another subsidiary label, Brunswick. At a stroke of his pen, Buddy Holly had the distinction of signing recording contracts both as an individual artist and as the member of a group.

It was, though, a moment of supreme irony—and one not lost on Buddy when he was told the good news. For both Coral and Brunswick were, in fact, subsidiaries of Decca! Buddy couldn't resist a laugh that came all the way from his heart.

'Hell, we had got in the back door after being thrown out of the front,' he said.

There can, though, be few other better examples in the record world of a company benefiting by a second chance after making an appalling blunder with the first. For when Brunswick released The Crickets' 'That'll Be The Day' on 27 May, 1957, it climbed steadily up the charts until it made the US Top Ten in August, hitting the number one spot on 23 September. That same month, released in Britain, the record moved rather quicker and occupied the top spot for a total of three weeks from 30 October!

A curious little piece of music folk lore has claimed that a single US disc jockey was responsible for the success of 'That'll Be The Day' by locking himself in his studio and playing the disc over and over again all through one day! Certainly, there *was* a d.j. named Guy King of WWOL in Buffalo, New York, who was very enthusiastic about the song and did play it an exceptional number of times on the air—but as to making it a hit on his *own*?

THE CRICKETS

CHARLES GOVEY introduces the new singing group sensation from Texas

from: *The New Musical Express*, Friday, 11 October, 1957

If somebody asks you where the hit records come from these days, you won't be far wrong if you reply: 'Deep in the heart of Texas.'

For the important Texan township of Lubbock has suddenly become the focus of the record industry through the activities of four young citizens who call themselves The Crickets.

And The Crickets, we need hardly remind you, have just chirped their way to the top of the American hit parade with a home-grown number called 'That'll Be The Day.'

This, their first release on the Brunswick label in the US, has hit the American charts for six by making its first entry at No. 7 and climbing to the top in four weeks.

It has already started repeating its success here for Vogue-Coral by reaching No. 9 in three weeks.

Started young

'That'll Be The Day' is certainly an all-Texan affair. Three members of the group were born in Texas, and the fourth has lived there for the past 17 years.

The key member of the group is 21-year-old BUDDY HOLLY. He started his musical career at the ripe old age of eight, when he began learning the violin. But a few weeks of scraping and squeaking convinced him that he wasn't going to be another Paganini, and he found himself much more at home on guitar.

At the age of 15, he started singing and playing at various clubs round the south west. Then one day he made a trip to Nashville, in Tennessee, the home of country-and-western music.

There he was heard by a talent scout

for Decca Records, who wanted him to record some of his own western material. Buddy was signed by Decca, but when his first two releases failed to make any impression his contract was dropped.

He returned home to Lubbock, convinced that there must be some other way of breaking into the recording field. He met another budding young musician called JERRY ALLISON.

Jerry, aged 19, is really a farm boy. He was raised in the small farming community of Hillsboro, and lived in various parts of Texas before his parents finally settled in Lubbock in 1950.

His first musical interests involved piano lessons at the age of six, but he soon changed his mind and decided upon drums as the source of his enjoyment.

Above: 'That'll Be The Day,' chorus The Crickets as they point to October 1, the day on which they expected to pass the millionth sale of their hit record. Helping The Crickets to celebrate this remarkable achievement is Bob Thiele, (*far left*), the a & r of Coral and Brunswick.

Jerry played drums at various clubs while still at school. But when he was offered a job with a group to tour the southern states, he left study behind in favour of becoming a full-time musician.

Friends

Then he met Buddy Holly. Both boys had a lot of ideas in common, and they quickly became friends.

They decided to form a musical group called The Crickets, and they wrote a song for the group titled . . . 'That'll Be The Day.'

They started looking around for suitable musicians to join the group, and found two right on their own doorstep.

One was a 20-year-old guitarist named NIKI SULLIVAN. Born in California, he has spent the past 17 years of his life in Texas. He has had a variety of odd jobs, but his main ambition was to make a career in music.

One day he was invited to go to the home of Buddy Holly, to watch some home recordings in the making. When he arrived, he was asked to join the group.

'Little fella'

For their bass-player the boys selected 18-year-old JOE MAULDIN, who, like Buddy, was born in Lubbock. Joe is known as the 'little fella' of the group, for he is quite a few inches shorter than the rest of The Crickets, who are all six-footers.

The starting-point for the new group was a trip to Clovis in New Mexico. There, the boys knew, was situated the finest recording studio in the entire south west.

The studios were owned by a technician named Norman Petty, a musician who recorded with his own trio and had penned a hit song, 'Almost Paradise.'

Petty saw the potential talent in the youngsters and took a special interest in them from the start. He became their manager, guided them through many hours of practice, and reshaped 'That'll Be The Day' into likely hit parade style.

At last he judged they were ready to make a test disc. The result of the session was sent to music publisher Murray Deutsch, in New York.

Deutsch passed the disc on to Bob Thiele, the a & r manager for Coral Records.

The next step surpassed the four youngsters' wildest dreams. Not only did Bob Thiele give Buddy a solo recording contract with Coral, he also decided to record The Crickets as a group on his subsidiary label, Brunswick.

Anyhow, the boys have little cause to complain. For under their new recording agreement, they not only record as a group for Brunswick, but provide the musical support for Buddy on his solo Coral discs as well.

Composers

This, combined with the fact that they write a lot of their own material, means that these young Texans aren't going to be short of cash for a long time to come.

The boys intend to provide for the future by investing some of their earnings in stock and bond companies. They also want to open their own music publishing concern, so that they can give fellow musicians and songwriters a break.

And like all true-blue Texans, they are proud to have put their home town of Lubbock on the entertainment map.

They'd certainly be happy if we in Britain began to associate Texas not just with cattle, oil and big buxom girls like Jayne Mansfield, but with the latest line in modern musical groups as well.

The simple truth is that this classic song, without the aid of record company hype and with very little media attention, caught the ears of rock 'n' roll fans across America—and, in turn, the rest of the world—and won their hearts by its sheer originality and brilliance. It was no more than Buddy Holly deserved in recognition of his persistence and determination.

Earlier, in June of that year, Coral had issued Buddy's first solo disc, 'Words of Love', backed by 'Mailman Bring Me No More Blues'. 'Words of Love' has a special place in the pantheon of Holly records because it was one of the earliest songs in which an artist sings with himself. Buddy believed the tune demanded two voices singing in unison, and because multi-track recording was then a thing of the future, he had to achieve this effect with a combination of Norman Petty's expertise at the sound mixing desk and his own ability to sing a tune twice using precisely the same words, inflection and timing. His achievement remains enshrined to this day on the track of that title.

'Words of Love' was not, though, the overwhelming success some histories would like to claim—primarily because a cover version was released at the same time by an established group, The Diamonds, who had just had a huge number one best seller, 'Little Darling'. Buddy was reportedly angry when he heard about this rival version, but because of the copyright law in America permitting artists to cover each other's songs as long as they paid the stipulated royalties, there was nothing he could do. In future, he vowed, he would make sure *his* versions were

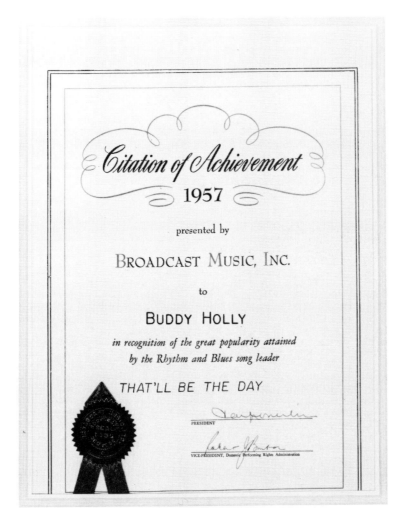

Citation of Achievement
1957

presented by

BROADCAST MUSIC, INC.

to

BUDDY HOLLY

in recognition of the great popularity attained
by the Rhythm and Blues song leader

THAT'LL BE THE DAY

PRESIDENT

VICE-PRESIDENT, Domestic Performing Rights Administration

Special award made to Buddy for The Crickets' first number one disc, 'That'll Be The Day', which was presented to him in October 1957.

first on the market. Time, though, has proved his record the classic, while The Diamonds' is virtually forgotten.

As a result of his efforts, Norman Petty became the manager of Buddy Holly and The Crickets by what is generally remembered as a kind of mutual consent. What was more important to the four musicians and their producer, however, was the thought that their agreement with Coral and Brunswick allowed them complete autonomy over the production of their records. Buddy now had the freedom to write his songs and see them performed as he wished.

Such overnight success—as it seemed to the world at large—of course made the four young Texans suddenly in demand everywhere for live performances. There were to be no more school dance hall dates or country club bookings for Buddy Holly and The Crickets. The big cities of America now beckoned, as did radio and television, while on the horizon lay still greater fields to conquer overseas.

First, though, there was another important little matter to deal with—the business of an image for the boys, a prerequisite considered of great importance in the world of show business. No longer would the casual open-necked shirts and Levis usually worn by the four young men in their performances be good enough. Buddy, however, was soon to get help with this problem from two Nashville singers who would not only influence the group's style of clothes, but their music also—Don and Phil, the Everly Brothers . . .

Changing All Those Changes

The success of 'That'll Be The Day' in the summer of 1957 transformed the lives of Buddy Holly and The Crickets. Now America was to become their oyster —and the first step towards this was signing up with one of the biggest booking agencies in the country, the General Artists Corporation in Washington DC, who were to catapult them from the school halls and dance clubs of West Texas to the theatres and auditoriums of the big cities across the continent.

Irving Feld, who took charge of the bookings of the four young men that summer, was inadvertently guilty of giving the impression that The Crickets were a coloured group when they set out for the East Coast on their first major theatre appearances. For because of their sound on disc and the fact that as yet no photographs had been widely seen of the boys, a number of promoters in Baltimore, Washington and New York assumed they must be a black vocal group! Feld, naturally, was happy to take the bookings for his new clients, and it seems very likely that neither he nor the promoters ever raised the topic of the group's race during the contract negotiations.

However, Buddy and his three friends soon discovered the misunderstanding when they arrived at their first date at the Royal Theater in Baltimore. One look at the posters outside the building told them they were the only white men on the bill—which included two coloured groups, The Cadillacs and The Hearts, and several fine black vocalists including Lee Andrews and Clyde McPhatter. Buddy, though, had worked too hard to be thrown at the first hurdle.

'Let's play a Bo Diddley number,' he told the other Crickets as they stepped out onto the stage at the Royal Theater to be confronted by a sea of dark, somewhat surprised faces. 'We'll give them a number to show we like black music as much as they do.'

And as soon as the boys struck up the famous Bo Diddley song that bears the guitarist's name, any hostility that might have been felt towards them quickly evaporated. Led by Buddy's driving guitar and his assured singing of the catchy lyrics, the others followed his example and played the very best way they knew. Later Jerry Allison was to recall this crucial moment in The Crickets' history.

'They were a really great audience,' he said. 'But it was tricky for us. I mean there were parts of Texas where the colour bar still applied and we'd never played to an all-black audience before. But there was no tension, and we really enjoyed it because black music was what we were in to.'

This first tour lasted just a week, but by the time they had played Baltimore, the Howard Theater in Washington and the Apollo in New York, Buddy and the boys knew their music did not just grab white boys and girls in the South, it had a more universal appeal, too. For apart from numbers like those of Bo Diddley, Little Richard's 'Ready Teddy' and Chuck Berry's 'Brown Eyed Handsome Man', they also did some of their own songs which lifted every audience to its feet. It was an exhilarating and exciting first taste of the big time.

Then, on 6 September, the group set out on their first nationwide tour, playing 80 different venues which would take them across the country and last until the end of November. This was to introduce Buddy and the others to the gruelling reality of life on the road—travelling by bus, sometimes hundreds of miles between dates, and without a day's rest in between. A constant round of play and pack-up, sleep when the opportunity arose (usually on the road for not many of the promoters were generous enough to book hotel rooms for such a large number of artists), and give 'em hell on stage.

The package, grandly titled 'The Biggest Show of Stars for '57', introduced the Texans to a number of other musical luminaries, for also along with them were Fats Domino, Chuck Berry, La Vern Baker, Clyde McPhatter, Jimmie Bowen, Frankie Lymon and the Teenagers, The Drifters and two other acts who would become Buddy's particular friends, Paul Anka and the Everly Brothers.

Of course, package tours like 'The Biggest Show of Stars' differed radically from today's live presentations which tend to feature a single top artist or group with no more than one or two guest artists as 'warm-up' performers. But in the glorious 'Fifties, packages of talent such as this offered fans the chance to see a whole clutch of top recording artists all at one time—though as no individual or group was allowed more than four or five numbers, waiting for a particular favourite could sometimes be a lengthy business. But as tickets rarely cost more than a few dollars, who was complaining?

At each city of the tour the artists gave two performances per night and earned on average $1,000 a day. Small potatoes in comparison to what today's rock stars can command, but riches to Buddy and the others after the $5–$10 they had been making for a whole night's work in the previous year or so!

Probably the biggest single attraction on this '57 tour was the Everly Brothers whose record 'Bye Bye, Love' had been the smash hit of the summer months. Of the two guitar-playing vocalist brothers, Buddy became closest to the younger, Phil, and it is not surprising, therefore, that his memories of the tour and Holly himself should be the clearer.

The Everlys were born in the small town of Brownie in Kentucky, the sons of two country music performers, Margaret and Ike Everly—their Dad better known as 'Cousin Ike' for his radio show broadcast from Ohio. Both boys had

music in their blood: Don, born in February 1937, was a radio star by the time he was seven, while Phil, born in January 1939, came to show business a little later as a result of his parents forming the Everly Family Show in the late 'Forties. This stage act was dissolved in 1954 and the two boys later trekked to Nashville in the hope of carving out individual careers.

Like Buddy Holly, the brothers had to endure an ill-fated recording contract with Columbia which resulted in a single, unsuccessful release. It was, though, a chance meeting with one of the leading 'Music City' agents, Wesley Rose, which led in time to a new contract with Cadence Records and a still more important meeting with the prolific and highly successful song writing team of Felice and Boudleaux Bryant. It was the Bryants who gave the Everlys their breakthrough song 'Bye Bye, Love', and after that history was made.

A few years ago, Phil Everly talked for the first time about his friendship with Buddy Holly—a friendship that remained warm and close until the sad day when Phil had to act as one of the pallbearers at Buddy's funeral.

'People have said that our style influenced Buddy Holly,' he said, 'but while it's true to say we did help Buddy and The Crickets get their clothes fixed, Buddy already had his style pretty well set by the time we met on the All-Star Show in September 1957.

Opposite: The Everly Brothers, Don and Phil, were to turn Buddy Holly into a picture of sartorial elegance! Below: 'Sometimes there were spats between the coloured guys and the whites,' Chuck Berry has said of the rock 'n' roll tour in which he and Buddy Holly co-starred in 1957. Scenes from the tour were recreated in *The Buddy Holly Story*.

'Now, I like casual clothes myself, but you just never did see anyone quite as casual as Buddy Holly when he started out! He'd been playing around these places where it really didn't matter what you wore so long as you could pick and sing. But it sort of made your whole act look dull if you came on a big show looking like that.

'Buddy once told me that he played some dates in Texas when it was real hot and he went on wearing Bermuda shorts! Most of the time it was jeans, a T-shirt and sneakers. Occasionally a long sports coat. For a bit he even copied Elvis and wore a red jacket. But the thing was he didn't really know *what* he wanted to look like.

'When the boys came on that '57 tour their manager had made them get some suits—but, man, you never saw anything like them! Pleat suits with cuffs and great big pants! So one day when we were all in New York I said, "Hey, you guys, you got to quit wearing that stuff and get some decent clothes." So we all went off to a store in the city [Alfred Norton in the Rockerfeller Center] and fixed them up with new clothes. After that they had pretty good taste—even Buddy—though he still loved lounging around in old jeans when he wasn't on stage.

'Buddy also used to wear these thin silver-rimmed glasses. One day I was joking him about them. I said, "If you've got to wear glasses, why not wear some real big ones?" It was half a joke, but instead of coming at me, a light sort of went on in his eyes. Later we went down to another store and got a pair of glasses with thick, black frames. They became his trade mark after that.'

Phil Everly not only influenced Buddy Holly's image, but also took a great interest in his music. For he, too, liked composing, and during the course of the tour he introduced Buddy to Boudleaux and Felice Bryant who had been so influential in his own career. The couple were also responsible for several of the Everlys' other big hits, including 'Wake Up, Little Susie', 'Bird Dog' and 'All I Have To Do Is Dream'.

Though the Bryants have only the vaguest recollection of Buddy Holly, they were to write a song with which he forever remains associated, 'Raining In My Heart', which Buddy recorded in New York in October 1958. (Among the Bryants' enormous repertoire of songs is also to be found one with the amusing title of 'Back Up, Buddy'—which, despite rumours to the contrary, has nothing whatsoever to do with Holly!)

'Buddy was not just a great singer but a fine writer, too,' Phil Everly said. 'Back in the summer of 1958 after he had become established, he tried to get Don and I to record two of his songs, "Wishing" and "Love's Made A Fool Of You". He cut some demos and played them to Wesley Rose in Nashville. Wesley said they were great songs, but he didn't think we should record them because nobody else's versions could be as good as Buddy's. It was a good thing those demos were saved and released after Buddy died.'

Phil Everly did, though, work on a recording project with his friend. In December 1958, Buddy wrote 'Stay Close To Me' for a new singer called Lou Giordano, while Phil wrote the 'B' side, 'Don' C'ha Know'. Though the record was issued on the Brunswick label shortly after Buddy's death and much was made in the publicity about the Holly association, it failed to make any kind of impact on the charts.

'The record wasn't a success,' Phil said, 'but if you listen to it you can sense Buddy had another talent apart from playing and singing. He could have made a good record producer, too.'

The Crickets' performance before an all-black audience with black groups at the Apollo Theatre in New York in 1957, as recreated for the musical, *Buddy*.

Producing records was still way off in the future for Buddy Holly and The Crickets as they and the rest of the package tour worked their eighty days across America in the Fall of 1957. But the trip was not all sweetness and light, as one of the artists, the great self-proclaimed 'Prime Minister of Rock', Chuck Berry, has recalled.

Berry, an object of enormous admiration among today's super stars of rock (John Lennon once said, 'If you tried to give Rock 'n' Roll another name, you might call it "Chuck Berry"'), was born Charles Edward Anderson Berry in October 1926 in St Louis, Missouri, and claims he arrived in the world singing. Despite an unsettled childhood—and three years in the Intermediate Reformatory for Young Men for some bungled robberies in Kansas City—Chuck discovered he had a talent as a musician who appealed to both black and white American teenagers in the 'Fifties and was soon an almost permanent fixture in the charts with songs like 'Maybellene' (1955), 'Roll Over Beethoven' and 'Brown Eyed Handsome Man' (both 1956) and the classic 'Rock and Roll Music' released in 1957.

'I spent most of '57 on the road,' Chuck has recalled. 'Irving Feld put together this thirty-one artist show which headlined me and Fats Domino and we played 72 one-nighters between February and April. The second version went out from September to November. Buddy Holly was on that tour. We went most everywhere on two buses, though sometimes I took off and travelled in my own car just to get a break.

'Most of the time things were pretty cool on the buses—we were just too damned pooped to fight. Buddy Holly liked to shoot craps so we would go up to the back of the bus while the rest of them were asleep and play for an hour or so. That guy had so much energy.

'Sometimes there would be a spat between one of the coloured guys and the whites. There were eleven acts and five of these were white. Someone said that Buddy Holly had an argument with La Vern Baker and she slapped him in the mouth.'

What the guitar maestro does remember vividly, however, is the racial tension he and the other artists experienced as their tour crossed America.

'We were what was then called a mixed show,' he said. 'A mixture of black and white artists didn't matter a damn in the north in places like the New England

Buddy Holly and The Crickets on the Ed Sullivan TV Show in December 1957. These rare shots from the programme show the group performing plus the individual artists, Niki Sullivan, Joe Mauldin, Jerry Allison and Buddy himself.

states where we could all stay in the same hotel and eat together. But it was a different story when we went south. Between Atlanta and New Orleans these police patrol cars actually stopped the two buses and made the black artists all get on one bus and the whites stay on the other. Hell, there were 96 blacks and just 20 whites!'

Chuck Berry remembers having to sit at the back of the bus a lot of the time and taking meals off paper plates while the others at the front ate off china; and theatres that were divided by race in the auditorium, though everyone—fans included—mingled back stage.

He was written of this period of his life, 'It was becoming clearer to me, upon returning to many of those southern cities, that the tension was mounting between the black and white people. But still the differences seemed to be hidden when they gathered for sports or music. As racially divided audiences were showing up to find mixed and open seating in the auditoriums, and with the security somewhat relaxed, the white fans visited backstage like we were all blue. Probably because of my rearing I noticed the friendliness of the white females more than that of the white males, going beyond normal musical appreciation to wanting to personally meet and associate with singers, something I never expected to occur.'

Rock 'n' roll, it might be gathered, was taking the first tentative steps towards helping break down racial barriers. But it was not just the coloured artists who suffered the brunt of intolerance. In a number of places the white performers were actually prohibited from appearing on the shows with their black colleagues. In Chattanooga, Columbus, Birmingham, New Orleans and Memphis, Buddy, the three other Crickets, the Everly Brothers, Jimmie Bowen and Paul Anka were all banned from appearing in the local theatres.

Several of those on this tour remember that Buddy Holly was furious about this segregation. He believed the laws were ridiculous, though he did allow himself a smile over the fact that The Crickets' record, 'That'll Be The Day', and Paul Anka's 'Diana' were then both in the Rhythm & Blues Top Ten!

On returning home at the end of the tour in November and being asked how he had got on with 'the negroes', Buddy is said to have replied, 'Oh, we're Negroes, too! We got to feeling like that's what we were.'

Buddy was not long in recovering his high spirits, and the month of December 1957 saw him climbing two more show business peaks. On 1 December, The Crickets made their TV bow on the prestigious Ed Sullivan Show which had earlier helped boost Elvis Presley to stardom when his notorious hip-shaking performance had stirred up a mighty controversy among viewers and critics. Buddy, however, peformed 'That'll Be The Day' and the recently released new hit 'Peggy Sue' without a hint of the lascivious, and was treated to a benign smile by a nonetheless rather unimpressed Ed Sullivan.

A second TV appearance followed in the week before Christmas on the Arthur Murray Dance Party, and then The Crickets were booked through the festive season on the famous Alan Freed 'Holiday of Stars' show at the Paramount Theater in New York.

Freed's Christmas Show was something of a legend in the Big Apple at this time as the showcase for the newest stars in pop music. It lasted for 12 days, invariably attracted huge audiences which created long queues outside the theatre, and sometimes the demand was such that as many as six two-hour shows would be put on during the course of a single day!

That Christmas package of 1957 certainly presented a dazzling array of talent, including Fats Domino, Jerry Lee Lewis, the Everly Brothers, Paul Anka, Danny and the Juniors, the Shepherd Sisters and Buddy and The Crickets. For the artists having to perform so many times each day was undoubtedly a tremendous strain, but at least there was no travelling at the end of the day and a comfortable hotel room awaited them each night.

There seems little doubt today that the Alan Freed Show was one of the high points of Buddy Holly's brief career. He and The Crickets then had three records in the Top Fifty—'That'll Be The Day', 'Peggy Sue' and the latest, 'Oh, Boy!' —and as the artists who received the most demands for encores, were probably the biggest draw on the bill. Certainly Buddy was in no doubt that he had made his mark—he was a STAR.

And unbeknown to him, the next stage of his career was already being finalised: a world tour to take in Australia and the country where his stardom was already growing enormous and, with the passage of time, would prove the most enduring—the British Isles . . .

Alan Freed's rock 'n' roll shows were smash hits with teenagers across America. Among the stars the disc jockey (*right*) presented were Buddy Holly and The Crickets and the great Chuck Berry (*left*).

'The First Gentlemen of Rock'

The year 1958 started with some good news and some bad news for Buddy Holly. The good news was that he and The Crickets were to make overseas trips to Honolulu and Australia and follow this by crossing the Atlantic to Britain, where it was evident their records were selling extremely well. The bad news was that Niki Sullivan had decided to leave the group.

Many explanations have been offered for this parting of the ways at the moment of The Crickets' greatest success. Personality clashes with Jerry Allison have been cited, although the drummer counters such stories by saying that Niki just wanted to leave because he did not relish all the touring that would now be demanded of a successful group in the public eye. The most likely explanation is that because Sullivan also happened to be an accomplished guitar player, a fine singer and no mean hand at song writing, he just hankered after a future where he could make a name for himself rather than be forever in the shadow of Buddy Holly.

Be that as it may, Niki Sullivan parted company from The Crickets without any show of grievance, and it is a fact that Norman Petty played an important role in getting the young guitarist a recording contract with Dot Records. There is evidence that the remaining members of the group debated about asking Sonny Curtis to return as their rhythm guitarist, but he, too, was on the verge of getting a contract and also held the same reservations as Sullivan about playing second fiddle to Buddy.

And so, not a whit less confident of their ability to make just the same sound as a much bigger combo, the trio decided to remain as they were. And while in New York in January for another spot on the Ed Sullivan Show, the three of them put

65

Opposite: Buddy ready for all kinds of weather on his world tour—including rain in Britain!

the decision to the test by recording two new songs at the Bell Sound Studios. The numbers were the classic 'Rave On' and—curiously and ill-advisedly—'That's My Desire', a number which had been a hit for Frankie Laine in 1947 but was hardly ideal material for The Crickets' particular style. Whatever the feelings of the group about this song, the first gave them such satisfaction that they at once returned to the road as a trio and never looked back.

It was on 28 January, 1958 that Buddy and his two friends left America for the first time as the stars of a package of talent which included Jodie Sands, Paul Anka and Jerry Lee Lewis who has to become another of Buddy's friends. They were on an auspicious mission as the first American rockers to tour abroad.

Jerry Lee Lewis, born in Ferriday, Louisiana, in September 1935, had graduated at Waxahachie Texas Bible Institute as a minister, but not long afterwards turned his fervent love of gospel music into one of the most explosive styles of entertaining ever seen on the stage. His earliest influence—like Buddy Holly's—was Hank Williams, although the piano rather than the guitar was his natural instrument. It was in the mid-Fifties, billed as 'Jerry Lee Lewis and His Pumping Piano', that he took to pounding the keys with every available part of his anatomy. And then with the release in 1956 of 'Whole Lotta Shakin' Goin' On' he became the rock legend he has remained to this day. Indeed, Jerry's very public private life of marital upsets, mysterious deaths, indulgence in alcohol and drugs, has earned him the nick-names of 'The Killer' and 'The Wild Man of Rock'.

Despite his awesome reputation, Jerry has one terrible fear that haunts him—flying. This fear, and the fact that it was to be the cause of Buddy's death, have crystallised his memories of his fellow performer.

'Yeah, me and Buddy Holly first got together to do the Alan Freed Show in New York 'round Christmas 1957,' Jerry told a group of journalists a few years ago on the anniversary of Holly's death. 'Started out with an argument we were all having with Freed about who should get top billing on the show. Fats (Domino) was being given the top billing, and both Buddy Holly and I figured we should have it as we'd had more hit records.

'Freed quieted Buddy and The Crickets down by paying them a bit more to stay put where they were and they agreed. That made Holly the highest paid act on the show, but money wasn't what I wanted. I told Freed, "I'm the King of Rock 'n' Roll and I can blow Fats right off the stage." Well, Freed wouldn't take no notice so I said watch out.

'An' I just went on stage in this white sharkskin jacket and red pants and tore the place apart. When Fats came on the people were gettin' up and goin' and he was dead. Afterwards he told Freed he wasn't going on again after me *ever*!'

Lewis remembers that Buddy Holly was the only other performer apart from himself to get requests for encores on the show. Because they had not been directly involved in the argument, Jerry and Buddy found themselves drawn together and—as Southerners and lovers of Hank Williams' music—discovered they had quite a bit in common. The rest of the shows passed in a euphoria of triumph for both of them.

Not surprisingly, then, when Jerry was approached to join the package tour to Honolulu and Australia with Buddy he accepted, albeit a little reluctantly.

'The reason was the flyin',' he said. 'I've always been afraid of aeroplanes and I knew Australia was a hell of a way off. But they got me with the money. The money talked me all the way there.' (As a matter of record, Jerry was paid $50,000 for the tour.)

Jerry Lee Lewis, the wild man of rock 'n' roll, who toured with Buddy and The Crickets in Australia.

The fact that this was to be the first tour of Australia by American rock 'n' roll stars may also have done a lot for 'The Killer's' ego: and it was a fact that was not lost on The Crickets, either.

Jerry and Buddy were reunited in Los Angeles before flying to Waikiki for a single date in Honolulu. Jerry's dislike of flying was not helped by the fact that he and his trio had not realised they would need vaccinations before they would be allowed into Australia, and a doctor had to be hastily summoned to carry out the necessary injections at the departure gate before the Emigration Officers would let them through! Fortunately, Buddy and The Crickets had got their jabs done earlier in Lubbock.

On the flight, Jerry remembered that both he and Buddy occupied themselves writing songs. And although no specific Holly composition is known to have

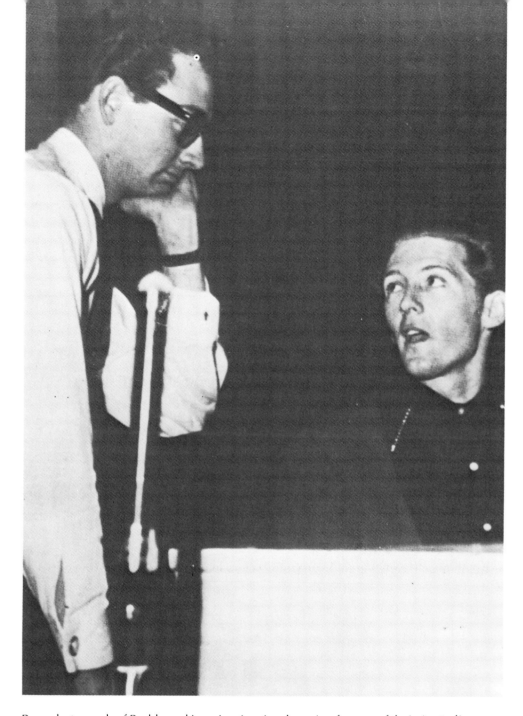

Rare photograph of Buddy and Jerry Lee Lewis rehearsing for one of their Australian concerts.

resulted from this flight, Jerry wrote most of the words and music for his very popular autobiographical number, 'Lewis Boogie'.

After a 12-hour flight the party of American rock stars reached Waikiki and were whisked off to the Hawaiian Village Hotel to await their evening performance at the Civic Auditorium.

'There were a lot of people turned out to see us in Honolulu,' Jerry recalls. 'And we were all over the newspapers. I remember Buddy and his boys tearing bits out of them about our visit. When we got to the hotel there were kids all over the place and we had to stay in our rooms until it was time for the show.'

The newspapers had, indeed, made much of the coming of the group of artists: one paper headlined its front page, 'ROCK 'N' ROLL REACHES HAWAII'. They also reported that the evening's concert was a complete sell-out.

All the musicians enjoyed the ground-breaking concert—from which considerable numbers of disappointed fans without tickets had to be turned away—and were equally delighted with the reviews the following day, which described rock 'n' roll as having 'made good'. An excited Buddy just found time to buy a postcard showing the picturesque Kaneohe Valley, and scribble a note to his sister and family back in Lubbock, before boarding the plane for the long haul to Australia.

'Hello from Hawaii,' he wrote. 'We played here last night and went over better than I thought we would. They like the same kind of music here.' And he signed the card with a hasty, 'Buddy'.

While the party was flying to Australia, Jerry Lee Lewis says he and Buddy talked a lot about the kind of reception they might receive 'Down Under'. Rock 'n' roll was now getting known all over the world, but the stories of youngsters rioting and wrecking auditoriums in America and Europe had gone ahead of them. Buddy didn't think he needed to worry on that score—although he reckoned he was generating his fair share of excitement when he performed —but 'The Killer' was quite another matter.

'Some of them Australians figured we were coming to tear the place apart,' Jerry recalls. 'They'd read about some of the things that had happened in the States with Elvis and reckoned we were all a bunch of wild men.'

In fact, though his choice of words may have been apt, the tour was to prove incident-free—at least in public for there *was* some spirited horse-play behind the scenes and during a trip into the Brisbane countryside—and the artists instead found themselves being described as gentlemen. Where Jerry's words proved apt concerned the Australian singer, Johnny O'Keefe, who was added to the package on arrival as he was then enjoying a big local hit with a record he had written himself, called 'Real Wild Child'! (As a matter of interest, during the tour Jerry Allison became very taken with this song, and on his return to America made a cover version which was released partially disguised under his middle name, Ivan, and backed with a comic version of the old standard 'Oh, You Beautiful Doll'. Buddy's opinion of this record was provided in just two words: 'A farce.')

The tour of Australia lasted seven days and took the package of stars to Melbourne, Sydney and Brisbane. In each city the demand for tickets was so high that extra concerts were played. An account of the tour written shortly afterwards by journalist Murray Silver says revealingly: 'Although each venue seated thousands upon thousands, second shows were added at every site to accommodate bushmen coming from the remote areas of the continent. It was possible that the performers would never see crowds of such proportions again.'

Jerry Lee Lewis remembered Australia best for the beer and the practical joke he played on Paul Anka—getting him drunk for the first time; while Buddy—a teetotaller—concentrated on giving the local fans a show they would never forget. This he achieved beyond any doubt, for although the tour of February 1958 was to be his one and only visit to the country, his personality and music made such an impression that to this day he remains one of the best known and loved of all American rock stars in Australia.

Reports of the tour differ in their opinions as to *who* made the biggest impact. Jerry's wild performances certainly won him many admirers at a number of the concerts, while the 17-year-old Canadian-born prodigy Paul Anka, riding the crest of his world-wide hit 'Diana', was certainly the favourite with many of the

Teenage sensation Paul Anka who appeared with Buddy in America and Australia and then had his own tour in Britain.

younger members in the audiences. But the foot-tapping brilliance of Buddy and The Crickets was perhaps most generally appreciated by *all* the audiences.

Indeed, John J. Goldrosen, author of a biography of Buddy Holly, has written that Jerry Lee Lewis himself—'in a moment of modesty'—told him, 'Buddy was the real star on that one—he just tore them up over there—just drove them wild.'

An Australian record executive, Ken Taylor, who also watched one of the concerts and met Buddy afterwards, shares this opinion. He wrote later: 'To meet him Buddy Holly was the perfect representation of a sombre American parson—ascetic, serious, dignified behind the horn-rimmed glasses he perpetually wore. His personality, innate decency—and talent—added up to an American legend. He was favourite and king.'

And as if he felt this praise was not quite fulsome enough, Taylor added: 'Genuine in outlook and unaffected in demeanour, Buddy and his group were the First Gentlemen of Rock.'

Though Buddy never read this tribute, the reviews of the Australian tour and

70

the fan letters he received while still in the country were enough to convince him that his music was, as he had always hoped and believed, international.

Further confirmation, if such was needed, was to come when, with hardly time to draw breath after flying back to America (and depositing a very relieved Jerry Lee Lewis on his native soil), Buddy and The Crickets turned eastwards and flew to Britain to open a four-week tour in London on March 1. (Coincidentally, Paul Anka also flew to Britain to open a 23-concert tour of the country beginning the same day in Aberdeen!) It was a trip the three Texans looked forward to with keen anticipation, for they knew their records had been even more successful in chart terms on this side of the Atlantic than in the USA.

Excitement about their arrival was also being generated in Britain, as a report that weekend by the leading pop columnist, Laurie Henshaw, of the *Melody Maker*, indicates.

Feature articles such as this one from the *New Musical Express* of 28 February, 1958, heralded the arrival of The Crickets in Britain.

Buddy Holly and the Crickets have been given a VIP greeting on their first visit to Britain. They have been booked straight into ATV's 'Sunday Night at the London Palladium' following their opening date at the Elephant & Castle Trocadero tomorrow (Saturday).

Decca's Coral label has also not been slow to pay tribute to the group that has paid off so handsomely discwise. Holly's new solo recording of 'Listen To Me' and 'I'm Gonna Love You Too' is out today. And the collective Cricket's offer 'Tell Me How' and 'Maybe Baby'—introduced on the Six-Five Special TV show last Saturday—the same day. Decca's Tony Hall has high hopes for the 'Baby' side.

Arriving with the Crickets at London Airport this afternoon—at 2.45 p.m.—is manager, Norman Petty. Holly and the boys understandably think a lot of Petty and they also pay direct tribute to Elvis Presley for 'paving the way' for their eventual success.

Probably only those of us who were alive in 1958 and fortunate enough to have seen the visit of Buddy Holly and The Crickets can appreciate the extent of the impact they had on the British music scene. Certainly by then Elvis Presley's records had indelibly imprinted themselves on our consciousness as, similarly, had Bill Haley's 'Rock Around The Clock' on the sound track of the 1955 movie, *Blackboard Jungle*. But they were *records*—Buddy Holly was the first American rock 'n' roll star actually to appear in the country's theatres.

For those fans not able to get tickets for the group's opening concert at the Elephant & Castle, Buddy and The Crickets were first glimpsed on the hugely popular TV show, 'Sunday Night at the London Palladium'. Collective excitement at seeing the trio overcame what was actually a rather poor performance. The reasons for this were threefold.

Firstly, because the show's technicians had never dealt with a group like The Crickets before, the volume and balance of the microphones were all wrong. Secondly, as a result of some fooling around in the dressing room before going on, Joe Mauldin had accidentally knocked the caps of Buddy's front teeth and he had to smear some chewing gum over them to disguise the damage, which naturally inhibited his singing. And, thirdly, the boys' anxiety to do well before their new fans led to some inadvertent mistakes in their performance.

But if anyone outside those in the know was aware of these faults, no one said anything—and from there on the tour through the country, going as far north as Newcastle and as far south as Southampton, was a sell-out success.

There was no question of the trio's star status—but the rest of the bill certainly seems a curious one to have supported a rock group, though it was fairly traditional by English standards of the time. There were three other singers: a female duo, The Tanner Sisters, a new British recording artist, Gary Miller, plugging his hit release, 'The Story of My Life', and saxophonist Ronnie Keene.

Backing all these acts was Don Smith and his Orchestra while the show was compered by Des O'Connor, 'the comedian with the modern style', to quote the programme.

O'Connor, born in June 1932 in Stepney, East London, and today one of the best-known comedians in Britain and star of his own TV shows, not only remembers that tour well but also has a very special souvenir to remind him of it—one of Buddy's guitars which he gave him as a present before leaving the country.

Opposite: Publicity photographs of Buddy and The Crickets associated their name with the English national game—and among those who attended the arrival of the group were two leading cricketers, Godfrey Evans and Denis Compton.

Des had a tough childhood in the East End: he had to wear callipers on his left leg because of rickets until he was seven, at ten he was run over by a car and at thirteen the family home was destroyed by a German bomb and they had to move to Northampton. He first worked with his father on a milk round, and was later an apprentice printer and worker in a shoe factory before discovering his talent for comedy and singing while in the RAF.

On his demob he started in showbusiness as a Redcoat at Butlin's Filey holiday camp, and made his professional debut in Newcastle in 1953. Thereafter he played in numerous variety shows up and down the country, before breaking into television and proving what a good voice he had by making the first of several hit records, 'Careless Hands'. Though Des O'Connor has been the butt of many other comedians' jokes over the years, his sheer professionalism, honed through tours just such as the one with Buddy Holly, have earned him the award of Favourite Male TV Personality on several occasions.

Apart from Buddy and The Crickets, Des is the only name from that tour to be remembered today.

'American rock 'n' rolls singers had a bit of a reputation for causing riots in those days,' he says, 'but I was ready for anything. I'd played in just about every music hall in Britain and everything had happened to me. When I was struggling to get started a crowd at Chiswick had rioted and thrown light bulbs at the stage. Another theatre had burned down and I'd had drunks climb up on the stage. So a rock 'n' roll riot would have been a doddle!'

In fact he remembers the tour as being exciting rather than dangerous.

'Buddy was actually just a tall, ordinary, fun-loving lad with a terrific sense of fun who talked like J.R. and couldn't get out of bed in the morning when we were on tour. But once he went on stage you realised you were in the presence of something very exciting. What we didn't realise was the mark he was to make on modern music.

'I used to watch him from the wings transfixed by the electricity of the guy—and 30 years on you only have to listen to some of today's music to realise that Buddy's legacy is still there . . .'

When they were not working, Des spent a lot of time with Buddy talking about life in Britain and about the various towns the show visited. They were forced to stay indoors a lot, he recalls, because it rained so much! He says Buddy described himself as just an American small-town boy still trying to get used to how quickly his life had changed.

'We had a lot of laughs together,' Des goes on. 'I saw him buying three Austin Healey cars. When I asked him why, he said he wanted to make sure he got a good one!

'He was always joking like that and great fun to be with. I used to write gags for him to tell on the stage and he used to get better laughs than I did with my own material! I believe he wrote home to his mother to tell her how the audience loved his gags and how he was getting bigger laughs than the Comedian on the show.'

As they travelled by coach from one venue to the next, Des remembers that Buddy used to play his guitar, a Hofner President acoustic, to while away the time. Des had, in fact, helped Buddy purchase this instrument when he arrived in London, as the tone of the guitar he had brought from America proved unsatisfactory.

'He would sing many standards, lots of new songs, and even composed some of his songs with this guitar. He would look out of the window, see something that

RONNIE KEENE

TANNER SISTERS

BUDDY HOLLY

DES O'CONNOR

GARR

Page from the programme of Buddy's British tour in March 1958 with co-star Des O'Connor. Right: Before flying back to America, Buddy presented Des O'Connor with his guitar in gratitude for the jokes which the comedian had provided!

caught his imagination and start to write a song about it there and then. At the end of the tour Buddy thanked me for the help with the jokes and gave me the guitar as a present.'

Des, of course, never saw Buddy again, but has kept the guitar as a memento of their brief but warm friendship. (The Hofner was offered at an auction of Buddy Holly memorabilia in London in April 1990 with an estimated sale price of £40,000–£60,000, but failed to reach its reserve.)

Whether or not Buddy did write to his mother telling her he was getting more laughs than Des O'Connor we do not know—but he certainly found the English weather no joke, as a surviving postcard he sent back to Lubbock reveals. Dated 14 March, 1958, and addressed to his sister Pat, the black and white card shows the Houses of Parliament, and on the back is scrawled:

> Dear Pat & Family, Just a few lines to say Hello. We are getting a little bit tired of England. It's awfully cold over here. Seems like it never could get Summer here. Well, so long for now. Love, Buddy.

By the standards of today's rock concerts with their laser shows, giant amplifiers and amazing sound systems, the performances The Crickets gave in March 1958 with their single guitar, a bass and a set of drums represented rock at its crudest. But such was the energy and electricity that the three young men generated on stage, that descriptions of them as 'fierce, blistering and exciting' were well merited. All the 28 performances followed a similar pattern.

Naturally, The Crickets were the highlight of the show. As soon as Des O'Connor had introduced them and left the stage, the curtains would sweep back and a wall of noise and the first chords of 'That'll Be The Day' would shatter the auditorium.

And there, before the amazed eyes of the audience packed tight in the darkness, stood this tall, gangling figure in black-rimmed spectacles. His fingers became a blur over his guitar as he leaped forward towards the microphone and began to belt out the words of the tune which most of those present had probably played a hundred—even a thousand—times on their record players. But not one of us had ever heard it quite like this before.

There was no time to draw breath, no time to take your eyes away from the dynamic trio up on the stage. The lights glinted off the faces of the two men behind the singer as they laid down the insistent beat of the familiar music. Then almost before the last line of 'That'll Be The Day' was finished, the trio were off again with 'Oh Boy!', to be followed by 'Peggy Sue'.

The *New Musical Express*, then the mouthpiece of rock 'n' roll, put into words what young audiences experienced at a Buddy Holly concert. 'It was a tremendous, belting, twenty-five minute act full of enthusiasm, drive and down-to-earth abandon,' according to the paper's critic Derek Johnson. And we all agreed with him.

We stamped our feet, sang along with the words, clapped and then cheered ourselves hoarse when, all too soon, the curtain fell and The Crickets had gone. No matter that some of the more fuddy-duddy national newspapers found the performances rude—suggestive, said one paper, of the lewd movements of Elvis Presley—for those of us who were teenagers in 1958 it was the vibrant music of youth that we had heard.

When we trooped out, exhausted but high on the music, into the cold London streets outside the Hammersmith Gaumont on the night of 25 March, we knew that we had seen Buddy Holly's last British concert and that the following day he would be off back to America. But neither I, nor anyone else for that matter, could possibly have imagined that it would be the last time he would ever play in Britain . . . and that within a year he would be dead and the legend of which the Australian writer, Ken Taylor, had written, would begin to be fashioned . . .

When The Fans Broke My Windows!

by Buddy Holly

From: *New Musical Express*, 28 March, 1958

Sitting on a table in his dressing room at Hammersmith Gaumont on Tuesday evening, Buddy Holly reminisced about the past 25 days in Britain and, breaking into a broad toothpaste grin, confessed happily: 'Sure, we had a real ball! It was just great!'

The remaining two Crickets—bassist Joe B. Mauldin and drummer Jerry Allison—nodded in agreement . . . then suddenly everybody was talking at once!

'The country as a whole is wonderful and the fans are real nice to us,' announced effervescent Jerry. Buddy cut in with an enthusiastic 'You bet!' and diminutive Joe B., perhaps the quietest member of this talented trio, just smiled thoughtfully and cocked a thumbs up sign.

Buddy took over for a while as spokesman to recall some of the interesting things that happened during the tour.

Glancing through a date schedule, he singled out the State, Kilburn, date earlier this month, and blurted out: 'You know what happened there? I broke a string for the first time! It kind of put us off-balance for a while, but everything went along fine when I got it repaired.'

At Southampton, he recalled seeing a lot of sailors in the audience at the Gaumont Theatre, and moving down the list to the Sheffield date, he added: 'We played at the City Hall, and it was pretty confusing because we had people sitting behind us. We're not used to that. And another thing, the weather there was cold, and dark, and dismal —I didn't like that.'

'You know, it snowed like mad when we played at Nottingham, and that wasn't too pleasant either,' said the bespectacled Mr Holly. Still thumbing through the schedule, he stopped at the date marked Birmingham, and looking slightly puzzled, asked himself: 'Now what happened there?'

'Oh, sure, I remember,' he exclaimed, as the quizzical expression vanished. 'We were taken round the Austin motor works, which was quite a big kick. We spent about half a day there going right from the foundries through to the assembly rooms.'

On the subject of fans, Buddy chuckled quietly and murmured: 'They were fine—nice, enthusiastic people, very receptive, and generally well behaved.

'**Mind you, some of them broke a couple of windows in my dressing room at Worcester trying to get autographs, but they didn't mean any harm.**'

Jerry Allison seemed eager to give his impressions of Britain, and he kicked off by saying: 'Well, it was just like we expected—lots of historic buildings and narrow little streets. It was sort of quaint in many ways.

'We were either working or travelling most of the time, so we didn't get a lot of time to ourselves. But when we were in London we got to see all the real important places like the Tower of London, St. Paul's Cathedral, Big Ben, Westminster Abbey and the Houses of Parliament. We saw the new Planetarium, too, but we didn't have time to go inside.'

About audiences, he concluded:

"Real nice people—even the Teddy Boys, with their long hair and sideburns! I enjoyed getting fan mail at the theatre every night, and always got a kick out of signing autographs. I reckon we signed our names about 2,500 times!'

Joe B. Mauldin occupied the speaker's chair to reminisce about the British entertainment scene. "In the States we usually tour with package shows that are made up entirely of rock 'n' roll acts. Here, we went out with a real variety show—comedians, ballad singers, jazz bands and rock 'n' rollers —and it made a nice change. I enjoyed it immensely!

'By the way,' he added, 'we like your Lonnie Donegan real good! We saw him at a midnight concert in London and he was great.

'Chris Barber and Ken Colyer were there, too. This was the first time I had seen any dixieland bands, and I don't really care for that kind of music. They played real well, though.'

The final shows at Hammersmith provided an incident worth mentioning. The Crickets bounded on stage to start their act, but Buddy's amplifier developed a fault, and the show was held up for a few minutes. Norman Petty, their manager, who was along for the tour, fixed it—and The Crickets exploded into action!

Rave On!

By the Spring of 1958 Buddy Holly was an acknowledged star on the world stage with several chart topping records to his name. Increasingly, too, he and The Crickets were becoming the focus of attention in both the music press and national newspapers in places as far apart as New York, London, Cape Town and Sydney. The contrast between the boys as performers and the wild antics of such as Elvis Presley, Jerry Lee Lewis and Little Richard were ideal topics for comparison—as well as elements to be discussed in the still raging controversy over the allegedly 'sinister' influence of rock 'n' roll on young people.

In April, The Crickets released a new record which remains to this day one of the seminal works of rock 'n' roll as well as one of the best known of all Buddy's discs, 'Rave On'. An astonishingly inventive number beginning with Buddy's repetitive shout of the word, 'well', it had been made by the trio at the Bell Sound Studios in New York back in January. The composers were Sonny West and Bill Tilghman who had produced the group's earlier hit, 'Oh Boy!'—and though the three young musicians were happy enough with the cut, they never imagined it was destined in time to become a cornerstone of the Buddy Holly legend.

There are those critics—and fans—who believe 'Rave On' to be the trio's most exciting record, and it is a strange fact that though this waxing is so well known, research has been unable to establish who provided the vocal backing for Buddy. What *is* known is that Norman Petty is the man on the piano.

Even stranger is the fact that despite their undoubted international popularity, 'Rave On' was, in comparison to their earlier discs, almost a failure for The Crickets on both sides of the Atlantic that Spring of 1958. In America, the record got no higher than number 39 in the charts, while in Britain, where the trio's tour

Opposite: Raving on . . . Buddy Holly the new international rock star in the spring of 1958.

was still fresh in everyone's mind, it only made it into the top five. 'Rave On' may therefore be another of those famous cases of a song's true stature only being recognised with hindsight.

However, if this record was a significant milestone in Buddy Holly's life, two other at least equally significant events were to occur in June 1958—both in New York City. Firstly, Buddy was to record without either Norman Petty or The Crickets; and, secondly, he was to meet the beautiful young girl who would become his wife for six short months. The two people central to both these events are still alive and have told their versions of the story.

The recording session took place on 12 June and produced two numbers, 'Early in the Morning' and 'Now We're One', both of which had been written by a young singer-songwriter, Bobby Darin. The producer of the session was the musical director of Coral and Brunswick Records, Dick Jacobs.

Jacobs, a genial man and an accomplished musician who plays a variety of instruments, regularly accompanied Coral artists on their recording sessions with his own orchestra. He was also something of a rarity among record producers in 1958, in that he actually liked rock 'n' roll rather than just recording it for purely commercial reasons.

'Though my musical upbringing had been with classical music, there was something so vibrant and exciting about what the young guys like Buddy Holly were doing back in the late 'Fifties that I was really glad to be a part of it,' he says. 'Of course we'd no idea we were making records that people would still be playing years later, but some of the best of them did capture the mood of the times. Teenagers were finding their own voices and expressing what they felt in music. I can still listen to a lot of the music of the 'Fifties and get a real warm feeling inside.'

Dick Jacobs also nurses a warm feeling for the memory of Buddy Holly, though he recalls that he was hardly over-impressed when he saw the young singer for the first time.

'The first time I met him was when he was appearing in one of those Alan Freed shows in New York. He was wearing these silver-rimmed glasses, and he had

Dick Jacobs of Coral Records, who helped Buddy develop his talent as a solo artist.

Actor Gary Busey looking very like Buddy listening to a playback of a recording session during the filming of *The Buddy Holly Story*.

gold-filled teeth and look like a hick from Texas. But when he came back later to record "Early In The Morning" what a change! Now he was wearing horn-rimmed glasses, a three-button suit and had got his teeth fixed. He looked a real gentleman—and he had the manners to go with it.'

Dick Jacobs also remembers the somewhat convoluted story of how Buddy came to record the two Bobby Darin numbers.

'Buddy and Norman Petty came up to my office in New York to talk about some future recordings and we got to discussing the music business in general. Buddy was always interested in what other young musicians were doing and somehow we got round to Bobby Darin—I guess because he was a composer and singer like Buddy.

'Now up to then Bobby had been recording for Atco but none of his songs like "Million Dollar Baby" and "Just In Case You Change Your Mind" had done anything in the charts and he figured the label was going to let him go. So he came along to see me and showed me these two things he'd written, "Early In The Morning" and "Now We're One". I liked them and so we did a deal to record them for release on the Brunswick label as soon as Atco dropped their option.'

Jacobs himself supervised the recording of the two songs with Darin which it was agreed would be released under the name of his group, The Rinkydinks. Then he sat back to let time take its course. But just before Buddy arrived in New York events had taken a very different turn. Atco had unexpectedly put out one final song by Darin—'Splish Splash'—and hit the jackpot. The record became a number one hit, sales topped a million, and Bobby Darin was a star.

'Of course, Atco weren't going to let us have him then,' Jacobs remembers, 'but I figured the songs could be recorded by someone else. It happened to coincide with Buddy being in New York and he agreed to do them. He didn't have The Crickets with him at the time, but I think he liked the idea of making a record on his own. Anyhow, he left it to me to make the arrangements.'

For the session, held only two days later, Jacobs picked some studios with the curious name of the Pythian Temple, which had a stage on which singers, musicians and, if necessary, whole orchestras could work together. To back Buddy, Jacobs hired a well-known local gospel group, the Helen Way Singers, brought in several of the musicians he normally used in his orchestra, and added two of the city's top session men, drummer Panama Francis and saxophonist Sam 'The Man' Taylor.

Dick Jacobs continues the story: 'Buddy liked gospel music and rhythm and blues so he felt comfortable with the line-up. He felt a real rapport with the Helen Way Singers and, of course, it was the first time he'd had a saxophone on a record.

'We played the Bobby Darin version of "Early In The Morning" a couple of times and then made three takes straight off. They were all good enough to release. Buddy had such a good ear. On all the songs I produced with him we never cut more than two or three takes at the maximum. And as far as his performance was concerned, we could have stopped right after the first take.'

There is no disputing that the second tune, 'Now We're One' was far less suited to Buddy's style—but 'Early In The Morning' became a personal favourite and on its release shortly afterwards ran the original Darin version very closely in the US charts, and actually eclipsed it in Britain, Europe and Australia.

The Pythian Temple session convinced Buddy—if he needed any convincing —that he could succeed as a solo vocalist in styles other than the rock 'n' roll which had made him famous. It may also have first put the idea in his mind that he could manage his own affairs. But now a little matter of the heart took precedence over everything else.

Buddy Holly had had girlfriends since his Lubbock days, and there had never been a shortage of female admirers when he began playing professionally. And certainly *not* once he became famous.

But when he walked into the offices of the Southern Music Publishing Company on Broadway that same month of June 1958, 'cupid shot his dart', to quote the words of his own song.

Buddy and the other two Crickets had an appointment with Murray Deutsch who was handling the publication of their songs. On arriving in the company's office they were confronted by Deutsch's darkly attractive receptionist, Maria Elena Santiago, a lively 25-year-old Puerto Rican girl whose aunt, Provi Santiago, was another of the company's executives. Maria had been living with her aunt since the death of her mother when she was eight years old, but had only recently moved to the music publishing firm after several other jobs in the Big Apple.

Maria Elena, who today has been married for close on 28 years to Joe Diaz, a Puerto Rican government official based in Dallas, and has three grown-up children, Carlos, Miguel and Elena, still vividly remembers her first meeting with the young rock star who was to sweep her off her feet and become her first husband. Understandably it took her some years to conquer the pain of Buddy's death so soon after their meeting and then the loss by shock-induced miscarriage of the baby they would have shared.

But time has healed the wounds and Maria Elena once again has the same infectious liveliness which first attracted Buddy, and she revealed this aspect of her character when talking about their brief but passionate life together during an interview given in 1979 after the making of the movie, *The Buddy Holly Story*.

'I have not forgotten Buddy, I could never do so,' she said, a broad smile

Buddy with Maria Elena Santiago whom he met and married in the summer of 1958. Also in the picture are Jerry Allison and his wife, Peggy Sue, the inspiration for The Crickets' famous song.

breaking out behind large glasses of the kind Buddy would surely have approved of. 'My husband Joe has said through the years that my love for Buddy and the time I spent with him were an important part of my life and I should keep his memory alive and be proud of it. My children don't make a big thing out of it, but all three have loved Buddy's music for years and they are very proud of their association with him. Joe has also encouraged me to tell them all about our life together. It made them smile when I told them how we met. They thought it sounded like something from a book, but it really happened this way!

'It was in 1958 and Buddy and the boys came in to see Murray Deutsch. They were like a lot of young guys in the music business and they couldn't resist fooling around. I'd seen it before and it was my job just to stay polite unless things got out of hand. I don't believe I took much notice of any one of them before they went in to see my boss.

'But when they came out, Buddy came right over with this big grin on his face and asked me when I would be free for lunch. I told him a couple of hours and he said, "OK, I'll see you around." I didn't think any more about it until one of the guys in the office asked me to go for something to eat at the Howard Johnson's across the way. When we got there they all were sitting with Norman Petty. Buddy had called this guy in the office and told him to get me down there.

'Anyhow, I had no choice but to sit with them and I ended up next to Buddy. For a bit they went on fooling around, playing footsie under the table and even trying to grab my hand. Then finally Buddy said, "OK, you guys, just cut it out. She's with me." And after we'd been eating a bit Buddy turned to the others and said, "You see this girl? I'm going to marry her. And she's going to agree before we leave New York!"'

Another smile crosses the face of Maria Elena at the memory of this dramatic courtship, and she admits that if there is a thing called love at first sight then that is what happened to her. For she had taken an immediate liking to the tall, gangling Texan with his big glasses. She sensed, too, that she *would* agree to marry him—but as someone who had not had much to do with boys, what would her aunt say?

Maria Elena Diaz, Buddy's widow, as she is today, with a photograph of the late star and one of his guitars. Opposite: Tommy Allsup, who joined Buddy Holly in New York in the autumn of 1958, pictured on the far right with his famous group, the Johnny Lee Wills Band.

In fact when Maria Elena merely broached the subject of going out with Buddy, Aunt Provi gave her a sharp lecture on the unsuitability of associating with musicians. But, conversely, when she asked her friends at Southern Music for their opinions of the young man she received a very different verdict indeed.

'Anyhow, I managed to convince my aunt that Buddy was all right and we went out to dinner at P. J. Clark's restaurant. And I know it sounds crazy, but he proposed before we had finished the meal. I thought he was joking and that made him upset. I said was he sure, shouldn't we think about it for a while? And he just said, "I don't have to think it over. I know I want to marry you." And so I said yes.'

Buddy now had to tell his own parents about his whirlwind courtship in New York. For a time he was apprehensive that they might object on religious grounds, since Maria Elena was a Catholic and he, of course, had been raised as a strict Baptist. Maria Elena remembers that her former father-in-law was welcoming and supportive from the start, and although there was a certain coolness from Mrs Holley this did not last very long—and, of course, they were all too soon to be united in grief.

The couple were married on 15 August, 1958 in a private ceremony at the Holleys' home in Lubbock by the family pastor, Ben Johnson, attended by a few friends. Among these were the two Crickets, Joe and Jerry who, as soon as the service was over, put on the record of 'Now We're One'. The new Mr and Mrs Holly only had time for a week's honeymoon in Acapulco before the demands of Buddy's career crowded in on him again.

The week had, though, been long enough for Buddy and his new wife to examine his career and decide some major changes were necessary. Maria Elena, with her knowledge of the music business, felt she could play a central role in the managing of his affairs and ensure that he was getting all the promotion, publicity and especially financial rewards to which his success entitled him. Buddy's idea about parting company from Norman Petty now became a definite decision.

He had also been mulling over all the satisfaction he had got from making 'Early In the Morning' and felt he wanted to write and record more ballads, perhaps even using a whole orchestra like that of his new producer, Dick Jacobs. Although rock 'n' roll was still dominating the hit parade, the public taste in music had always been fickle and if an artist did not want his career to come to a dramatic end when tastes changed, then he began looking for new directions before that happened. Which, with hindsight, is precisely what Buddy Holly did.

During the months of August and September 1958, in between their touring dates, Buddy and The Crickets recorded several more numbers for Norman Petty in Clovis including 'It's So Easy', 'Heartbeat', 'Wishing' and 'Reminiscing'. For these tapings, another bass player, a Clovis session man named George Attwood, was added to the line-up along with a brilliant lead guitarist, Tommy Allsup, whose contribution to the Buddy Holly legend has been sadly neglected in most accounts—though the man himself remains modestly unperturbed by the fact.

Allsup, who was born in Tulsa, Oklahoma, in 1931, had grown up with a wide-ranging interest in music, from the homegrown Country & Western to jazz and the classics. His talent proved to be on the guitar and as a teenager he was already playing in local groups. By the time his path crossed that of Buddy Holly in the summer of 1958 he had been the lead guitarist of the popular Johnnie Lee Wills Band for several years.

Tommy arrived in Clovis one July day to play at a recording session, and his

virtuosity as lead guitarist so impressed Norman Petty that the studio boss invited him to stay on and work as a regular session man at Nor Va Jak. Buddy Holly happened to visit the studios shortly afterwards, while Allsup was playing, and saw in a moment exactly why Petty thought so highly of the musician from Tulsa. After a discussion with Petty, Buddy asked Allsup if he would play with The Crickets on record and also appear with them at their live performances. Tommy was happy to take up the offer, and though, inexplicably, his name did not appear on The Crickets' records nor was he billed on stage, for a time he effectively made the group a quartet once more.

Today, Tommy Allsup still works as a session musician in Nashville, and remembers his brief association with Buddy Holly as just one chapter in a busy and happy life.

'Around the time I met Buddy he was getting very interested in different kinds of music because he wanted to expand his knowledge and experiment with new styles. I remember we talked a lot about jazz and he even bought some albums. He was interested in Cajun music, too, in particular the records of Rusty and Doug (Kershaw) from Nashville who were then being handled by Elvis' first manager, Bob Neal. Buddy thought about spending some time learning Cajun music which I believe would have suited his style. I reckon that those ballads he started making just before his death would have only been the first step towards all sorts of new things.'

Rusty and Doug Kershaw, two Cajun singers, whose music was influencing Buddy Holly in the last months of his life.

Tommy has also never forgotten Buddy Holly the man.

'He was one person on stage and a quite different one off it,' he recalls. 'He always worked hard on stage to get through to the kids and he could tear up an audience. But off stage he was very quiet—he just liked to sit around with the other musicians and talk—usually about music.'

The ballads to which Tommy Allsup refers were the four he cut with Dick Jacobs in New York in October 1958. (Allsup also has a special reason for remembering the tunes as he later made an instrumental version of one of them, 'True Love Ways', and it remains among his favourite recordings to this day.) But though no one could possibly have known it at the time, this was to be Buddy Holly's last recording session. What he committed to tape at that session is now tinged with a mixture of poignancy and sadness.

The session was again booked by Dick Jacobs at the Pythian Temple, though this time Buddy's only accompaniment was to be the producer's own orchestra. Buddy did not even play his guitar as he vocalised his way through 'True Love Ways', 'Moondreams', 'Raining In My Heart' and 'It Doesn't Matter Anymore'.

The first two numbers were Holly/Petty collaborations, while 'Raining In My Heart' had been penned by Boudleaux and Felice Bryant. The last of the quartet was the handiwork of Buddy's young touring companion, Paul Anka, and had just been completed that day. It was only included in the session at Buddy's insistence and some last-minute arrangement by Dick Jacobs, as the producer himself has explained.

'We had been having these discussions all day about the string session,' he says. 'Then about five o'clock in the afternoon Buddy came into my office with his guitar and said, "Paul Anka just played me the most fantastic song in the world. We have to do it tonight." I said, "But the session starts in three hours!"

'And Buddy says, "We *gotta* do it. Please, you gotta write an arrangement. You gotta do it." So I called my copyist—he came right in—and in three hours we had a string arrangement ready on "It Doesn't Matter Anymore" which, of course, turned out to be the big hit of the session.'

That record is famous for two reasons. It is the first rock 'n' roll record to feature a string accompaniment; and, secondly, it is Buddy Holly's soaring, unforgettable finale as a singer. Nor has the similarity of the lyrics to those in the last record made by Buddy's hero, Hank Williams, in his 'I'll Never Get Out Of This World Alive', gone unnoticed by critics or fans.

But from such moments are legends made. And the final act in the legend of Buddy Holly was now less than four months away . . .

Cold Days . . .
and a Black Night

It was on Tuesday, 28 October, 1958 that Buddy Holly decided to break with his mentor, Norman Petty. It was also the day when he and The Crickets parted company, too, and the trio of young men from Lubbock, Texas—Buddy, Jerry and Joe—broke up their partnership that had shaken the rock world and created some of its most enduring records. The road to fame they had travelled had been hard, fraught with setbacks and upsets, but ultimately triumphant.

The date was, though, merely one of convenience. The group had completed another cross-country Alan Freed tour co-starring with Eddie Cochran, Bobby Darin, Frankie Avalon, Clyde McPhatter and The Coasters, and also made a guest appearance on the prestigious Dick Clark TV show, 'American Bandstand'. Those fans who saw Buddy Holly and The Crickets on what was their last television appearance remember how assured they now looked and how much they had matured since the Ed Sullivan appearances just a few months earlier. Maybe some of their youthful exuberance had gone, but in its place was professionalism of the highest order as they showed all the other performers how to rock, playing a medley of their best known numbers.

Buddy and Maria Elena had now decided on settling in New York where the musical action was—in a high rise apartment block in Greenwich Village—and though there is evidence that Buddy wanted Allison and Mauldin to continue working with him (Tommy Allsup did, in fact, remain in New York until the following spring) his two partners instead decided to return to Lubbock and plan the next phase of their careers with Norman Petty, with whom they had no axe to grind.

The reasons for this dissolution of one of the most famous pioneer rock 'n' roll

89

Opposite: One of the last photographs taken of Buddy Holly in New York in January 1959.

bands have been endlessly argued over, with blame being apportioned to each of the musicians in turn, as well as to Norman Petty, Maria Elena Holley, artistic disagreements and booze. Today such arguments seem pointless and futile —though they do still go on—in the light of the tragedy which lay just on the horizon.

That the three musicians could have succeeded by going their own separate ways seems entirely likely—as their great admirers, The Beatles, subsequently demonstrated—though Jerry and Joe allowed themselves to be convinced by Norman Petty that they should remain together because, he said, it was the collective Crickets who were actually famous rather than the individual Buddy Holly. This the two friends have done throughout the succeeding thirty-odd years and, supplemented by several changes of partner, have continued to appear as The Crickets occasionally in America but more regularly in Britain. (A tour of the current Crickets, Jerry, Joe and Gordon Payne, with co-stars Duane Eddy and Tommy Roe, was actually in progress through England and Scotland in April 1990 as I was completing this book.)

In New York in the winter of 1958, Buddy busied himself planning for the future, working as an independent record producer and taking drama lessons at the famous Lee Strasberg Actors Studio—for making a film was very much on his career agenda. Two new records were also released in October and November, 'It's So Easy' backed by 'Lonesome Tears' and 'Heartbeat' with 'Well All Right', the latter aimed at making an impact on the Christmas market. Buddy was also enjoying being a newly married man—though Maria Elena sometimes found it hard to keep up the pretence to fans that she was just Buddy's secretary!

In fact, Maria Elena had now taken it upon herself to be responsible for the promotion of Buddy and his music: answering fan letters, organising fan clubs and taking her rather reluctant husband along to a New York photographic studio to get some publicity shots taken. One of these photographs provided the cover illustration for the first posthumous album, *The Buddy Holly Story*, released in April 1959. Not without good reason has this picture (illustrated here) been described as making the young singer look just like a rather serious concert pianist!

January 1959 began with a burst of creative energy from Buddy holed up in his New York apartment. He had made a new agreement with Dick Jacobs about his future recording plans and also decided upon setting up his own music pub-lishing company, using his wife's name as the title: Maria Music. He was also feeling good after a trip to Lubbock at Christmas to see his parents and some old friends, so that when he and Maria Elena returned to the Big Apple, the 22-year-old star was soon scribbling furiously and making demonstration tapes of a number of his new compositions.

Speaking some years later about this fateful last month in her husband's life, Maria Elena said, 'We spent a lot of the time listening to records while we did the chores or sat around in the apartment. Buddy liked music on all the time as he was always getting ideas from what he heard. He was never afraid of learning from what other people were doing, and I got him interested in Spanish music. He became fascinated by flamenco guitar music and sometimes we even sang Spanish songs together. We put a few of those songs on tape but I'm sorry to say they have got lost.'

What were not lost, however, were the songs that Buddy himself had written and sung into a tape recorder in the couple's living room. Played today, complete

The Buddy Holly Story

The famous 'concert pianist' pose of Buddy used on the April 1959 album, *The Buddy Holly Story*, and the poster for what was to prove his last performance.

with the overdubbing which was added later, these tunes clearly underline what an accomplished writer he had become and hint at the directions in which his talent was taking him. The six numbers are: 'Crying, Waiting, Hoping,' 'Learning The Game', 'That's What They Say', 'What To Do', 'That Makes It Tough', and that evocative sequel song, 'Peggy Sue Got Married'. (As a matter of record these tunes were actually overdubbed *twice*: firstly in New York that same year, with instrumental and vocal backing by Jack Hansen and his Combo; and a year later in Clovis by Norman Petty, with the accompaniment of a Texas group called The Fireballs who had scored a chart success with a number called 'Sugar Shack'. In all honesty, The Fireballs' backing is far closer to the spirit of The Crickets than Jack Hansen's mood music style.)

Tommy Allsup, who was living in New York in January 1959 working mainly as a session man, says he accompanied Buddy on some of these demonstration discs (in particular 'Peggy Sue Got Married') and remembers the high note of optimism on which his friend was working. The only cloud on Holly's horizon, says Allsup, was a financial one.

Since the split from Norman Petty in October, Buddy had been waiting for finalised accounts of the royalties owing to him under his agreement with his former record producer. These could have been complex enough because of copyright and legal problems if Buddy had only been a solo artist, but as part of a trio and co-author with one and sometimes more than one other song writer the accounting became more tortuous still. In the interim, Buddy's existing funds had naturally become severely drained.

Since the split-up, Buddy had received several offers to make solo appearances on shows with his old friends like Jerry Lee Lewis and Paul Anka, but he was not keen on the arduous travelling that would be involved, nor on being separated from Maria Elena as they were hoping to start a family. (In fact, by January the young Mrs Holley was confirmed to be pregnant.) It has also been suggested that he was concerned about appearing without The Crickets and still nursed a hope that they might all get back together again. But needs must when money drives, and when Buddy was approached in the middle of January by Irving Feld to join a 'Winter Dance Party' package of rock 'n' roll musicians being set up to tour the Midwest, he agreed.

It is quite clear on looking at the supporting acts for this tour that Buddy Holly was the one *established* star, and it is perhaps equally true that but for the tragedy

J. P. Richardson, 'The Big Bopper', one of the other ill-fated passengers with Buddy, in typical rumbustious style on a television show in 1958, and (*left*) young Los Angeles singer Ritchie Valens who also died in the plane crash.

which followed, few of the other artists would still be famous today. The party actually consisted of five acts: four singers—Buddy, Ritchie Valens, J. P. Richardson known as 'The Big Bopper' and Frankie Sardo—and a group, Dion and the Belmonts.

Two of the artists could, though, boast recent hit records: 'The Big Bopper' with his novelty tune 'Chantilly Lace', and the teenager Ritchie Valens who, like Paul Anka before him with 'Diana', was then at number two in the charts with a number about *his* girlfriend called 'Donna'. Fate was shortly to make them both part of the legend of Buddy Holly . . .

Jiles Perry Richardson was another Texan like Buddy, born in the small town of Sabine Pass in October 1930, the son of an oil field driller. The family later moved to Beaumont in Texas where young J.P. went to the local High School and proved himself an outstanding footballer. Along the way he jettisoned what he considered his embarrassing first name for the more appealing Jape.

Blessed with a tremendous sense of humour and a personality that got him referred to as a big cuddly Teddy Bear, J.P. took up playing the guitar and singing while in the Army where he served for two years as a radar instructor. On his discharge, he landed a job as a disc jockey on KTRM in Beaumont, and after he had noticed a number of teenagers doing a dance called The Bop, decided to host his evening record show as 'The Big Bopper', a gimmick which was to help make his name.

In May 1957, J.P. earned himself a curious place in the history of rock by creating the record for continuous on-the-air broadcasting when he occupied the microphone at KTRM for a period of five days, two hours and eight minutes and played a total of 1,821 records! Richardson had also begun to compose songs, and after a number of moderately successful releases on the Mercury label wrote 'Chantilly Lace' which broke into the charts in the summer of 1958 and remained there for 22 weeks, going as high as number six. Among his other numbers which were later successfully recorded by other artists were 'White Lightnin'' which was a number one C & W hit for George Jones in 1959, and 'Running Bear' (based on stories he heard as a child about the Red Indians in his native Sabine Pass) which his friend Johnny Preston got to the top spot in the pop charts just before Christmas 1959.

It was the continuing success of 'Chantilly Lace'—plus the chance to promote his new record, 'The Big Bopper's Wedding' released in December 1958—which encouraged J. P. Richardson to get a leave of absence from his job at KTRM and join the others on the 'Winter Dance Party'.

The life story of the other headliner, Ritchie Valens, was much less dramatic. Born in Los Angeles in 1942 of Mexican parents whose full family surname was Valenzuela, Ritchie had been strongly encouraged to sing right from infancy. At High School he won a talent contest with a song he had written himself, and at the age of 16 he began pestering local record companies to let him make a disc. His dark good looks, which got him compared to the popular film star Glenn Ford, made an executive at one Hollywood company take notice.

Ritchie's first recording, 'Come On Let's Go', however, made little impact (though, ironically, it was to become a success for Britain's Tommy Steele the very month Valens died), but with his second number, the plaintive appeal to his girlfriend 'Donna', he became an overnight sensation when the release shot up the charts to number two. Ritchie had already recorded a follow-up, 'La Bamba', based on his Mexican heritage, which would also become a hit—but not until after his death. He had been maintaining to everyone that he was 21 years old and it was only after the accident, when the facts were checked, that it was learnt he was actually just 17 and had only left school the previous autumn!

There were no thoughts of disaster in Buddy's mind, though, as he planned for the tour, though with his dislike of the cold he was concerned about just how bitter the Midwest was going to be. In February, towns in the states of Wisconsin, Iowa, Minnesota and North Dakota, where the 'Winter Dance Party' was to tour for three weeks, were usually in the grip of ice and snow and all forms of motorised transport had to battle through freezing conditions and snowstorms. It was the thought of the tremendous reception which artists braving this terrible weather invariably got from the rock 'n' roll loving fans of the Midwest that kept most of them going.

Buddy obviously needed a supporting group for the tour, and naturally enough first invited Tommy Allsup who was happy to get the work. He next telephoned Niki Sullivan, but the former Cricket declined the invitation. So in his place Buddy hired Waylon Jennings, a disc jockey at KLLL in Lubbock, who played bass guitar and would later become a big star in the country music field; plus a drummer, Charlie Bunch. Although this combo was billed by the promoter on the posters as The Crickets, this was not authorised by Buddy and neither did he refer to them as such during his brief spell on the fated tour.

One of the survivors of the tour, Dion Di Mucci, the leader of Dion and the Belmonts, remembers those February days with awful clarity—and the fact that it was probably only the lack of the price of an air ticket that prevented him from joining Buddy and the other two artists on their doomed flight.

Born of Italian stock in the mean streets of New York's Bronx district in July 1940, Dion began to develop a love of music and singing when he was given a guitar as a birthday present. By the age of eleven he had made his first professional appearance on the Paul Whiteman Radio Show and at seventeen formed his first group which he called The Belmonts. Although the band's first disc proved a failure, the boys persevered and the follow-up, 'I Wonder Why', was a hit and earned them the booking on the 'Winter Dance Party'. If 'earned' is the right word.

'It can get pretty cold in New York, especially when you're a hungry young kid like I was,' Dion Di Mucci said recently in New York where he still performs regularly. 'But that winter tour when Buddy died was just about as bad as any I can remember. It was so cold one of the guys actually got frostbite and had to be left behind in a hospital.

'We travelled by bus, sometimes four or five hundred miles between dates. In the first week one of the buses just died on the road and we had to switch to another in the nearest town. There was never any heating in them and you had to fool around to keep warm. Getting some sleep was a real problem.

'What kept me going was the thought I was going to earn some real money at last. At that time my parents were paying $35 a week renting a flat in New York. It might not have seemed a lot of money to someone like Buddy who was already a star, but it was to me and so I was prepared to stick it out in the bus. The money from those dates was too precious to think about using on plane tickets . . .'

Dion's memories of the dates the party played before they reached the small town of Clear Lake in the north of Iowa on Monday, 2 February, are of freezing bus rides broken only by the enthusiasm of the youngsters who crowded in to see them in the ballrooms and dance halls they played. Everything comes into sharper focus for him after the 350-mile drive on the Sunday evening from Green Bay, Wisconsin, to the lakeside resort.

'We got held up for several hours that Sunday night when the damn bus broken down in the snow again,' he said. 'By the time we got to Clear Lake it was only a couple of hours before the show was due to start at the Surf Ballroom. We always went on early, so we barely had time to clean up before we were on.

'We were all getting pretty fed up with the conditions, but none of us wanted to let the kids down. After all they'd come from miles around to see us. So despite the fact we were cold and tired we gave them a real good time, Buddy as well. Funny thing was, though, that night he didn't sing his latest release "It Doesn't Matter Anymore".'

Dion says that after the show Buddy Holly told the other artists he couldn't take another night on the bus and he had chartered a light aircraft at Mason City Airport—which was about ten miles away from Clear Lake—to fly to Fargo, North Dakota, near Moorhead, the next date on their agenda. Tommy Allsup and Waylon Jennings were going with him, he said.

'Seems Ritchie Valens and J. P. Richardson talked the other two into letting them have their seats somehow and booked themselves tickets to death. I didn't hear the news about the crash until we got to Fargo. It was devastating. It didn't really sink in for a day or two. Then I saw Buddy's Stratocaster guitar which had come by bus and it just blew me away. It was awesome, especially when I thought I could have been on that plane, too.'

Di Mucci, who gradually overcame his grief and later made several hugely successful solo records, including 'The Wanderer', 'Teenager in Love' and, with a nod of acknowledgement to Buddy Holly, 'Runaround Sue', believes rock stars all over the world owe a debt to the Texan.

'He gave a lot of us the confidence to be singers who did something other than croon like Frank Sinatra,' he says. 'And if I can still make it at 50, I'm sure Buddy could have done so, too . . .'

The story of the last flight of the four-seater single engine Beechcraft Bonanza plane, flown by the comparatively inexperienced local pilot, 21-year-old Roger Peterson, which left Mason City shortly after 1.50 a.m. carrying the three entertainers, and crashed within a matter of minutes on a frozen farm field about ten miles away, is now a part of history. As are the two stories of premonition of the disaster.

The first concerns Buddy himself. He is said to have told the manager of the Surf Ballroom, Carroll Anderson, when he asked him what his ultimate ambition

Daily Mirror

WED FEB 4 1959

FORWARD WITH THE PEOPLE
No. 17,150

Tragedy of 'Jape' Richardson—

THEY CALLED HIM—

BIG BOPPER

TOP 'ROCK' STARS DIE IN CRASH

From HARRIE HARDING, New York, Tuesday

THREE of America's top rock 'n' roll stars were killed in a plane crash today, a few hours after delighting teenagers at a "big beat" concert.

The Clear Lake Mirror-Reporter

NUMBER 2

VOLUME 90   CLEAR LAKE, IOWA, THURSDAY, FEBRUARY 5, 1959

DEATH OF SINGERS HERE SHOCKS NATION

Rock 'n Rollers, Pilot Die in Tragic Plane Crash

The wreckage of the single-engined Beechcraft Bonzana aircraft in which Buddy Holly died on 3 February, 1959 . . . and two of the newspaper headlines reporting the tragedy to readers in America and Britain. Below: *New Musical Express* report of the second tour that was never to be.

NEW MUSICAL EXPRESS

NOW IT CAN NEVER HAPPEN, BUT

Buddy Holly package show was coming here

CLIFF'S SORE THROAT
LEAVES 'OH BOY!'

was: 'Well, I'm either going to go to the top—or else I'm going to fall.' The other less substantial story is that Maria Elena had a dream the night before Buddy left on the tour, in which she saw him dying in a big ball of fire that rushed through the air.

By the morning of 3 February, the tragedy at Clear Lake was on its way to making headlines across the United States as well as internationally. (Reports from the *Clear Lake Mirror-Reporter* and Britain's biggest selling paper, the *Daily Mirror*, are reproduced on page 95 as typical of many such accounts.) For other musicians—and fans—the news was unbelievable, devastating. Buddy's touring companion, Paul Anka, rushed into print with an intimate and deeply felt tribute which is reprinted here for the first time; while one of the star's biggest fans in Britain, Marty Wilde, another rock 'n' roller who had been inspired by Buddy, spoke the thoughts of millions.

'To any kid in the street Buddy Holly came as a godsend,' he said. 'You could look like an average kid from any small town and still become an idol.'

The singer Don McLean, in his famous song 'American Pie', described that grim February event as 'the day the music died'. For Buddy Holly the end had certainly come too soon with still so much to do. But he *had* had time to break the mould and his influence was to reach far beyond the grave. Far from his music dying, both it and his legend were just beginning to live.

And thirty years on they are still growing . . .

Paul Anka, a close friend of Buddy Holly, wrote one of the warmest tributes to the singer a week after his death. It is reprinted opposite.

MY BUDDY

**One famous recording star pens a heartfelt memorial to another great star
by PAUL ANKA**

from: *New Musical Express*, 13 February, 1959

If only Buddy Holly had made that last fateful journey by coach, instead of allowing his impulsive desire for speed to take possession of him, the tragic circumstances of his death would not have occurred.

Ever since I first met Buddy (and we have in all played about 150 engagements together), he has been dominated by a perpetual yearning for excitement and adventure. He enjoyed water ski-ing and swimming; was mad about motor-cycles and fast cars.

But it was flying that gave him the greatest sense of satisfaction, partly because overland journeys made him impatient, and he was looking forward to the day when he could obtain a licence and learn to fly his own aircraft.

They say that appearances are deceptive and Buddy certainly confirmed this.

Offstage he was for ever modest and retiring. Seldom did anything ruffle him. He always struck me as the type more likely to be found serving in a hamburger bar or delivering the soft drinks.

Opposite

Although he gave this impression of being quiet, his performances on stage created just the opposite effect! He derived tremendous enjoyment from making live audiences revel in his music.

Now he is gone—cruelly, prematurely—and the show business world is the poorer.

I shall always cherish the memory of the deep friendship which grew up between us, although for the moment the bitter reality of last week's shattering disaster has completely overwhelmed me.

The news hit me even harder because I was not told of the tragedy until I arrived at London Airport on Saturday evening, direct from my Italian tour. I refused to believe it until I bought a copy of the NME, which verified that frightful fact. Since then I have scarcely been able to control my sorrow and dismay.

You see, Buddy and I were very close.

We both achieved national success at about the same time (Buddy and The Crickets reached the top with 'That'll Be The Day' immediately before my 'Diana' took over), we shared the same agent and we toured extensively together.

In fact, you may remember that last year Buddy and I both undertook British tours, which opened on precisely the same day, March 1!

The last song that Buddy recorded before his death was a composition of mine, bearing a title which now seems bitterly ironical—'It Doesn't Matter Anymore.'

I feel specially unhappy for Buddy's widow, Maria, who—to the best of my knowledge—is expecting a baby. Buddy's marriage was a very happy one, even though the ceremony itself was kept quiet, presumably because Maria is Puerto Rican, which could have aroused a certain amount of controversy and perhaps scorn in America.

Even I did not know about the wedding until Buddy phoned me just after the ceremony had taken place!

He met her, by the way, in the New York offices of the Southern Music Company, where she worked as a telephonist. And not long ago, she and Buddy moved into their brand new home in New York's suburbs.

It is difficult for me to write about Buddy's business affairs for these he kept very much to himself.

The general impression was that the breakaway from his manager, Norman Petty, and the other members of the original Crickets was inevitable several months before it actually happened. Nevertheless, although something of a foregone conclusion, Buddy was still deeply concerned about having to take this step.

It was widely believed that there was a degree of bad feeling on this last, ill-fated tour. Buddy had engaged two new men, billed as The New Crickets, while the original group (also on the bill) had teamed up with another singer, who was regarded as the closest possible counterpart of Buddy Holly!

Because the original Crickets performed early on in the programme, they were able to take their pick of the big numbers the group had made famous.

So Buddy's presentation was restricted, but this did not seem to deter him in any way.

Buddy spent all his spare time concentrating on writing songs and developing this aspect of his career. I think he felt it was a sound, long-term policy.

Jam session

Of course, he was also an extremely proficient guitarist. One of his great delights, whenever the occasion permitted, was to get together with instrumentalists from other groups with whom he was touring, to form a sort of gigantic jam session.

He always used to say that people like himself owed their success to Elvis Presley, who was the pioneer and champion of his kind of music.

But for all that, Buddy had a distinctive individuality of his own and I line up with your own Tommy Steele, whom I saw quoted as saying: 'He had the sort of voice that every coffee-bar singer liked to try to imitate.'

Buddy Holly had something rare among artists—an even, placid temperament, which made him equally as pleasant off-stage as on.

More than that, his climb from obscurity to stardom had not affected him in the slightest, and he remained the genuine good-natured person he was at the outset.

As an artist, he was one of the most outstanding I have ever encountered and I can honestly say that he was one of the nicest guys I ever had the pleasure of meeting.

Believe me, I do not write these glowing words merely because of the sad occasion. This is a very sincere last tribute to someone with whom I had plenty of time to become friendly and to admire a great deal.

Not Fade Away

Despite the fact that Buddy Holly enjoyed only a few brief years of fame, so remarkable were the elements of his reputation that since his death he has proved a great attraction to film and TV programme makers as well as radio and stage producers. In the thirty years which have passed his legend has undoubtedly been reinforced by productions in all these four media of entertainment.

Although it is sadly true that only a few brief sections of video film of Buddy taken for television still exist, there were at least two movies he might have starred in. And as the making of films about his life has been beset with problems, so tracking down the facts of the Holly legend in the entertainment media has proved, as I found, both complex and revealing . . .

The first clue to Buddy in the movies was provided by Jerry Allison who said, 'We had a couple of offers for movies, and Norman (Petty) turned them right down—they were just rock 'n' roll movies, and I guess Norman was right waiting for the really big one. But that turned us right off, because we wanted to see ourselves in the movies.'

Buddy, of course, on several occasions expressed his desire to appear in films, and when he and Maria Elena settled in New York during what were to prove the last months of his life, as we have seen, he began going to classes at the Lee Strasberg Actors Studio where, he knew, many famous film stars had learned their craft—including two of his heroes, Marlon Brando and James Dean. Based both on what he said—and the evidence of Jerry Allison—it seems that Buddy Holly would have liked to appear in the two movies offered to Norman Petty.

It was in 1956 that the film *Rock Around The Clock*, starring Bill Haley, The Platters and Alan Freed, started the trend for featuring prominent rock 'n' roll

99

Opposite: Buddy the stage performer—he also planned to become an actor in films.

Jerry Lee Lewis starred in *Jamboree* (1957) in which his friend Buddy should also have appeared.

stars in films. Few of these films had any pretentions to storylines, but set out to offer audiences maximum exposure of the current chart-toppers they featured.

Aside from some clearly exploitive pictures made in the immediate aftermath of *Rock Around The Clock*, which was said to have caused rioting at many cinemas where it was shown (these movies included *Shake, Rattle and Rock*, *Don't Knock the Rock* and *Rock Pretty Baby*), the second important movie in the genre was *Jamboree*, released by Warner Brothers in 1957. Buddy Holly and The Crickets were to have been among the stars.

The producer of *Jamboree*, Milton Subotsky, who later became a leading independent producer in Great Britain, told me, 'The idea we had was to have a group of DJs across the US and Canada introducing as many of the top rockers as we could line up. It only meant a couple of days filming for most of the acts, and we just brought them into the studios and put them before the cameras and had them do their latest hit records.'

Among the performers Subotsky and director Roy Lockwood lined up were several of Buddy's co-stars from the Alan Freed package shows, including Fats Domino, Jerry Lee Lewis, Buddy Knox, Jimmy Bowen, Carl Perkins, Slim Whitman, Frankie Avalon, Connie Francis and Count Basie and his orchestra. All tastes catered for!

And Buddy Holly? 'Yes, we wanted him because he was pretty big then with "That'll Be The Day", but his manager turned us down,' said Milton Subotsky.

The second movie was *Go, Johnny Go*, made by Hal Roach in late 1958 but not released until April 1959. Alan Freed was the actual star of this picture as a DJ very like himself, trying to promote the career of an up-and-coming artist named Johnny Melody. Chuck Berry led a pack of rock 'n' rollers who guested in the movie, among whom should have been Buddy and The Crickets, then with a string of hits behind them. Again, Norman Petty rejected the offer from Roach Studios—and Buddy's last chance to make a film was gone.

One of Buddy Holly's keenest British fans was the first man to begin the creation of the Holly legend in show business not long after the star's death, when he launched a weekly pop music show using Buddy's song title, 'Oh Boy!' This pioneer 40-minute weekly rock programme, which began on 30 May, 1959, was the brainchild of Jack Good, recently described as 'the British high priest of pop and rock music programmes on both sides of the Atlantic'.

Born in London in 1930, Good graduated with a degree in philology from Balliol College, Oxford (where he had been President of the University Dramatic Society) and entered television as a trainee producer at the BBC on their very first pop show, the 'Six-Five Special', in 1957.

'Elvis and Buddy Holly were the first rock singers who grabbed me,' Good admitted years later, 'and although we had some great guys in England like Cliff Richard and Marty Wilde, they never quite matched the Americans. When I left the BBC and went over to ABC to create a new rock programme for them in '59 I decided to call it after Buddy Holly's song. It just blew my mind the first time I heard it.'

'Oh Boy!' remains as a landmark in British television, and no viewer was ever in any doubt as to the source of its inspiration. A review of the programme written in 1979, when the series was being revived, said, 'Oh Boy! was a pop television legend—the blending of a rock 'n' roll show with an enthusiastic audience created a magic experience for TV viewers, achieved through a breathless pace and rapport amongst the performers. Cliff Richard and Marty Wilde demonstrated the huge debt owed to American pop in general and Buddy Holly in particular.'

Jack Good was undoubtedly primarily responsible for keeping the Holly flame alive in Britain in the years immediately after his death, regularly using fans of Buddy's music on his show—among them Cliff, Marty, Billy Fury, Dickie Pride and Cricket look-alikes, The Dallas Boys. Often these artists sang Buddy Holly

Above: Jack Good, a Buddy Holly fan, who did much to promote the legend on BBC Television's weekly show, *The Six-Five Special*, and then in his own landmark TV programme, *Oh Boy!*

David Essex, who starred in the film based on Buddy's famous song, *That'll Be The Day* (1972).

compositions as well as their own records.

He also tried to use the title when he moved to America in 1962 to produce a similar show for TV, but had to settle for 'Hullaballoo'. When Jack returned to Britain in 1979 to revive his show for ATV, the generic title of 'Jack Good's Oh Boy!' was given to the weekly programme and he again featured Holly admirers, such as guitarist Joe Brown and singer Alvin Stardust.

There was an undoubted hiatus of interest in Buddy Holly in films and on television until the early 'Seventies—but once revived it gathered speed and has never looked back.

In 1972, *That'll Be The Day* was the title of a British movie written by Ray Connolly and produced by David Puttnam, which captured the spirit of the late 'Fifties of which Buddy was such an integral part. The film starred David Essex, who had just come to public notice starring on the London stage in the musical, *Godspell*, and who also happened to be a Buddy Holly fan.

Set in the year 1958 when a new generation of British kids was beginning to rebel against many of the attitudes of their parents, *That'll Be The Day* was about Teddy Boys, their stilettoed girlfriends, and the fun fairs, coffee bars, and holiday camps which were the 'in' places to go. But most of all it was about the impact of rock 'n' roll on young people. As film critic Gavin Millar of *The Listener* pointed out in his review, 'Jim Maclaine (David Essex) is so taken up by Elvis, Buddy Holly (hence the title), the Everlys, that he ends up buying a guitar which he's no more likely to master than he did his A levels.'

David Essex was on the verge of his teens when rock 'n' roll arrived and he admits it had a profound effect upon his life.

'I was into gangs and going into pubs and gambling and I could well have ended up a villain,' he says. 'But I got hooked on music and formed a group. We all liked Buddy Holly and The Crickets.

Dancing to 'Maybe Baby' in Francis Ford
Coppola's nostalgic movie, *American
Graffiti* (1974).

'I was the drummer, but as mine was the only voice that had broken I became
the singer as well. Then people came along waving contracts under my nose.
They said I should quit the band and they would make me a star. But I stayed with
my mates until the group finally broke up of its own accord.'

In *That'll Be The Day*, David is similarly saved from a life of villainy after
leaving home when he meets a pop star Stormy Tempest, the leader of 'The
Typhoons' (played by Billy Fury) and decides on a life in music. Another rock
star, Ringo Starr, appeared as his friend, Mike, and the picture was studded with
music from juke boxes which included several records by Cliff Richard, Tommy
Steele, the Everly Brothers and, of course, Buddy. (In 1974, the same production
team made a sequel, *Stardust*, set in 1963, with David now the leader of a super
group called 'The Stray Cats', who ends up disillusioned and dies in his Spanish
Castle retreat of a drug overdose.)

Two of Buddy's songs, 'Maybe Baby' and 'That'll Be The Day', as well as The
Big Bopper's 'Chantilly Lace', were featured in Francis Ford Coppola's production, *American Graffiti*, directed by George Lucas and released in 1974. A
highly praised movie, it was set in Modesto, California, in the year 1962 and
dealt with the lives of four teenage boys on the night before they are about to
leave their small town homes and go East to college. During the course of the
evening, they are confronted in a hamburger joint by the local drag race
champion, Big John Milner (Paul Le Mat), who is something of a ladies' man and
much envied by the others. After listening to a record by the Beach Boys, Milner
delivers a verdict which is very much the core of the film:

'Rock 'n' roll's been going down hill,' he says, 'since Buddy Holly died.'

The success of this comedy drama started a profitable run of early-Sixties
nostalgia in both films and on TV, culminating in the long running and very
popular TV series, 'Happy Days', which starred Henry Winkler as 'Fonzie', a

young man not unlike Buddy Holly—minus the glasses!

In 1975, the first attempt to make a film about Buddy Holly was instituted by 20th Century Fox. There is evidence that other companies—including MCA-Universal Pictures, ABC-TV and several independent producers—had considered filming his life story, but had been unable to obtain the permission of all those involved, or else failed to raise the necessary finance. Initially, the 20th Century Fox project, entitled *Not Fade Away*, looked to have a fair chance of being made.

The idea for this film had originated with Jerry Allison who still fretted that he and Buddy and Joe had not had a chance to go before the cameras back in the late 'Fifties. With this in mind he wrote an outline of one of their ten-day tours in the American South during the early days of their fame. Jerry knew he was treading on dangerous ground, because this was the tour when they had been the only white group among the touring acts and had encountered some hostility both on the bus and in a few of the small towns they played. But he felt this was an important element in the story to show how such racialism had later been swept away by the universal appeal of rock 'n' roll.

Fox did assign a screenwriter-director to the project, Jerry Friedman, and another singer from Lubbock, Joe Ely, was auditioned to play Buddy. Preliminary filming even began in Texas, but two weeks into the schedule and with principal photography looming, 20th Century Fox closed down the picture.

In an interview, Jerry Friedman claimed that it was the racialist nature of the script which caused the film company to withdraw their support.

'*Not Fade Away* would've been a damn right-on movie about rock 'n' roll,' he said. 'The storyline had The Crickets headlining the shows but getting hassle from the black groups on the bus journeys and from their predominantly black audiences. Jerry Allison told us that was the way it was, and we figured there was no Buddy Holly story if we ducked the issue. Fox weren't prepared to go along with that.'

Other alternative theories for the shutdown of *Not Fade Away* have been advanced, but the simple truth remains that Jerry Allison's story has not—yet—reached the screen.

Two further movies were to be linked to the legend before a life story was, at last, brought to the screen.

In 1975, director Robert Altman produced his wonderfully evocative but at times savage study of 'Music City', *Nashville*. If Buddy had lived it would doubtless have been a picture he would have enjoyed with its study of the stars and the no-hopers of country music. Filmed in the same Nashville streets he had walked during his ill-fated recording period with Decca Records, the movie further established Altman as one of the greatest modern directors.

Altman, in fact, had been interested in the music scene for years—back in 1950 he had made a film called *Corn's-A-Poppin*, about a gawky young country singer (played by Jerry Wallace who later had a Top Ten hit record with 'Primrose Lane' and became a popular C & W artist) who inadvertently finds fame singing a popcorn commercial. The film maker was also interested in rock stars, and in 1961 cast Fabian to play a charismatic drifter and murderer in the TV series, 'Bus Stop'. Altman came to public attention with *The James Dean Story* in 1957, and there are unconfirmed rumours that he was for a time one of the independent producers interested in making a film of Buddy's life.

Be that as it may, it is interesting to note that one of the songwriters on

Gary Busey looking uncannily like Buddy in *The Buddy Holly Story*, filmed in 1978.

Nashville was Gary Busey, who wrote the lyrics and music for one of the movie's numbers, 'Since You've Gone'. Three years later he was to become the first actor to portray Buddy on the screen . . .

Just before this, in 1977, Buddy's music was featured in Paramount's *American Hot Wax*, produced by Art Linson and directed by Floyd Mutrux. The film was a tribute to Alan Freed and his part in battling the authorities who wanted to close down his rock 'n' roll shows. As several of Buddy's contemporaries appeared in the movie, including Jerry Lee Lewis and Chuck Berry, is it unreasonable to think that if he had still been alive he would have starred, too? Several of the actors were praised for their roles, including Tim McIntire as Freed, Laraine Newman as an aspiring songwriter, Jeff Altman as a hustling record promoter, and Moosie Drier as a 'Buddy Holly groupie', to quote the *Variety* review!

In 1978, *The Buddy Holly Story* was finally made as a result of the persistence of three independent film makers, executive producer, Ed Cohen, producer Fred Bauer and director Steve Rash, who achieved their dream after years of negotiations, in particular with Buddy's widow. Starring Gary Busey as a remarkably life-like Buddy, and hailed by critics as 'a superior musical biography', the picture received both Oscar and Golden Globe nominations, Busey himself winning the accolade of Best Actor of the Year from the National Society of Film Critics. According to the *Sun*, the film was also responsible for getting underway 'an astonishing Buddy Holly revival on a new wave of nostalgia'.

The picture was notable because, unlike most musicals, it did not rely on pre-recorded synchronisation techniques: all the music was staged, performed and recorded live on the sound track. This was made possible because Gary Busey and his two co-stars playing the other members of the trio, Don Stroud (as Jesse) and Charles Martin Smith (Ray Bob), were accomplished musicians and could duplicate Buddy and The Crickets almost perfectly. The group were not able to call themselves The Crickets in the film because of the earlier agreement between Jerry Allison and 20th Century Fox, and Norman Petty did not appear by name, either.

In praising the picture, John Coleman of the *New Statesman* drew an interesting comparison between Buddy and an earlier star. 'Mr Holly of the big capped teeth and horn rims (eerily reminiscent at times of Harold Lloyd's go-getting college boy) is well impersonated physically by Gary Busey who picks the guitar and howls the ballads.'

Though the picture undeniably took liberties with some aspects of Buddy's life, it has an importance above and beyond such criticisms, as Dave Marsh pointed out in a very perceptive review in *Rolling Stone*.

> Even though it follows only a vague outline of real life, *The Buddy Holly Story* strikes me as an important movie. Its best scenes show Holly struggling for control of his sound. Nearly everyone wanted to water it down, make him more pop and less rock—which is certainly true to life. I believe that rock 'n' roll is somehow separate from the rest of the entertainment business. *The Buddy Holly Story* helps me understand why. To put it most simply, today's rock musicians have more direct, personal control over their work than novelists, broadcasters, moviemakers or any other toilers in the popular arts.
>
> This wasn't always true—there were those who wanted things to be done according to formula and one of Buddy Holly's greatest contributions was his involvement with every step of the record making progress: production, arranging, writing and as one of the pioneers of the overdub, even engineering.
>
> In a way it's this part of Holly's vision that is his greatest legacy. Today, rock musicians are free to spend months in the studio trying to craft perfect recordings without much corporate interference, in large part because of battles fought by such earlier musicians. Holly helped to contribute to rock the notion that it was possible to do it all, no matter what anybody said. And while it is true that those who made *The Buddy Holly Story* probably had *The Glen Miller Story* in mind as a model—Miller was, after all, another pop musician with glasses who died in an air wreck—that larger vision shines through.

Gary Busey himself had a vision, too, about how to play Buddy on screen, and found himself under the spell of the singer during the making of the picture.

'It was like living with a ghost from the 'Fifties,' Gary's wife Judy has since explained. And in the next section of this book, 'A Modern Don Juan', Gary himself talks about the role in fascinating detail.

If he had lived, Buddy Holly would have been 50 in 1986, and the anniversary of his birth was marked in Britain by a television special and in America by the making of a new film utilising another of his famous song titles.

The TV production, 'Buddy Holly', screened on 5 September, was created by producer Anthony Wall of the BBC 2 weekly programme *Arena*. To celebrate the

Nicholas Cage and friends giving a passable imitation of a rock group not unlike The Crickets in *Peggy Sue Got Married* (1986).

anniversary, the programme director Richard Spice filmed in Lubbock and conducted interviews with people who had known or been influenced by Buddy. Among these were Jerry Allison, Joe Mauldin and the Everly Brothers, plus Britain's top rockers, Paul McCartney and Keith Richard who explained how their respective groups had both recorded Holly tunes among their very earliest discs.

A highlight of the programme was some amateur film of Buddy on tour and at home with The Crickets, plus some unique footage of Elvis Presley performing in 1956. The hour-long special delighted viewers and critics alike, the *Daily Mail* describing it as a 'a definitive profile, sad and fascinating'.

The film underway at this same time was *Peggy Sue Got Married*, another nostalgic journey back to the 'Fifties—this time with elements of fantasy —directed with style and panache by Francis Ford Coppola for Tri-Star Pictures. It proved to be a 'beguiling package pickled in the music of Buddy Holly', to quote Angela Branki of *Today*—which was hardly surprising as both the scriptwriters, Jerry Leichtling and Arlene Sarner, confessed to having been raised on the late star's music.

Starring as Peggy Sue Bodell was Hollywood's latest sex siren Kathleen Turner who, while preparing to go to her old High School's 25th class reunion, suddenly finds herself magically back in the body of the 18-year-old cheerleeder she used to be while retaining the mind and memories of the 40-year-old housewife she was at the beginning of the story. This time, though, she has the chance to put right what has gone wrong with her life, and in particular the man she married and is now thinking of divorcing.

Kathleen Turner, also a Buddy Holly fan, went to considerable lengths in studying the time period in which the story was set and even unearthed one of her own High School prom dresses to play her younger self. The result was that she accurately personified the Peggy Sue of Buddy's song, and the film understandably established her as a force to be reckoned with among American actresses. Credit was also given to Nicolas Cage as her husband, Charlie Bodell; Barry Miller as Richard Norvik, a bookish, aggrieved science whiz; and Kevin J. O'Connor as a Kerouac-spouting beatnik, Michael Fitzsimmons.

An even more personally felt tribute to Buddy was the television film *Words of Love*, written by Philip Norman and shown on BBC 2 on 29 January, 1989. The story counterpointed the final hours of Buddy Holly in Clear Lake, Iowa, against the life of a schoolboy across the Atlantic on the Isle of Wight, who is modelling his troubled young life on that of the rock 'n' roll star.

The story was, in fact, very much Philip Norman's own—as the novelist and biographer of The Beatles and The Rolling Stones admitted at the time of the screening. He had, he said, first heard the name of Buddy Holly while 'snogging in the dark' with his girlfriend Sheelagh in the winter of 1957, as they listened to records being played on Radio Luxembourg by the ex-boxer, Freddie Mills.

The hypnotic drumbeat of 'Peggy Sue' captivated the young Norman, and he became even more intrigued when he learned that Buddy Holly was not your average handsome pop star.

Original illustration by Alan Baker for Philip Norman's short story, *Words of Love*, which was adapted for BBC Television in January 1989, starring Pancho Russell (*right*) as another look-alike Buddy Holly.

'While Elvis and the rest were wild, complex and remote,' said Norman, 'Holly seemed modest, intimate and intelligible. Especially to middle-class boys nervous of rock 'n' roll's toughness and squalor, he was the first vaguely possible role model. If you happened to own a guitar, as I and thousands like me did, Buddy Holly became, quite simply, your best friend.'

Philip Norman remembers feeling 'a faint flatness' when news of Buddy Holly's death reached him on the Isle of Wight, and it was only during the next few years that he became fully aware of the extent of Holly's influence on rock, as well as the magnitude of his loss to music. It was Anthony Wall's *Arena* documentary which really opened his eyes to what Buddy Holly had been like as a person: 'a character very different from our parent's anti-rock 'n' roll propaganda.'

Philip Norman continued, 'I then had the idea of writing a story alternating between myself on Ryde Pier and Buddy Holly in Iowa in the hours leading up to his death. The gulf between the two hemispheres was, after all, one that his music constantly crossed and re-crossed. For a link I chose "Words of Love", most brilliant of all the Holly songs that failed to make the charts.'

The author said that in discovering the truth behind the legend he found Buddy to have been charming and thoughtful, understanding, honest and true. 'A friend well worth having,' he added.

The story was brought to the screen by producer Brian Eastman (recently acclaimed for his Hercule Poirot and Jeeves series on TV) and directed by Colin Nutley. The excellent cast was headed by 16-year-old Charlie Creed-Miles as Philip Norman's doppelganger, Ivor Seaford-Warwick, with James 'Pancho' Russell as Buddy.

Russell, an Anglicised American born in Texas 25 years ago, had been working in England on the stage and in television when casting for *Words of Love* was announced.

'Of course Buddy Holly is more of a legend in Britain than he is in the States,' says Russell, 'but I'd heard his music and the chance to play the part of an American in a British production really attracted me. Actually it was the role of Ritchie Valens that I went after—but as soon as I tried on Buddy's black-framed spectacles at the audition they said the likeness was uncanny and offered me the part!'

Uncanny the likeness certainly was—and much commented upon by viewers and the national newspaper critics. Peter Paterson of the *Daily Mail* was one of this number and also gave a special mention to Tom Bell playing Ivor's sneering father 'whose idea of wit was to ask what his son could possibly see in someone called Bloody Holly.'

There were also noteworthy performances by Nadia de Lemeny as Maria Elena Holley, Bradley Lavelle as The Big Bopper, Paul Birchard as Tommy Allsup, William Jongeneel as Ritchie Valens and Mark Zingale as Dion. The story was painstakingly filmed against the winter landscapes of Cromer while the famous Art Deco Hoover Factory in London was cunningly used to evoke America in the 'Fifties. The production was, as Peter Paterson said, 'memorable, sentimental and rather touching'.

Memories were also evoked a week later on BBC Radio 1 when the thirtieth anniversary of Buddy's death was marked with an hour-long programme, 'Not Fade Away', produced by Kevin Howlett and presented by Alan Freeman. In recent years, radio stations in America, Britain, Europe and Australia have presented programmes acknowledging Buddy's contribution to modern music, most of them consisting of playing his records. 'Not Fade Away' was considerably more adventurous than these, being based on interviews with Buddy's mother, his widow, his producer Norman Petty and friend Jerry Allison—interspersed, of course, with his music.

Appropriately, perhaps, the anniversary was marked with the news that Buddy was at last to be celebrated in the one remaining entertainment medium his legend had not yet reached—though he himself had been its master—on the stage. This was the musical, *Buddy*, written by Alan Janes, directed by Rob Bettinson, with Bruce Welch of The Shadows as musical consultant.

Janes, formerly an assistant manager to The Who, had studied acting and writing and contributed to numerous TV series, including *Z Cars*, *Grange Hill* and *Minder*, before working on his authentic version of the Buddy Holly story. The production mixed a recreation of Buddy's rise to fame against performances of all his famous songs, to which the audience were invited to sing along.

Director Rob Bettinson, with a string of successes in both the theatre and television behind him, flew to New York to search for an actor-singer to play the leading role. He found four possibles and, after conducting similar auditions in London where he picked another quartet, brought all eight together for a jam session at the Royalty Theatre on 17 July. They had been whittled down from over 200 applicants.

Bruce Welch, who admits that Buddy Holly was one of his earliest influences as a guitarist, sat in on this session to pick the star. Bruce's special interest in the casting was heightened because of his years of working with his Holly-lookalike friend, Hank Marvin in The Shadows, and by Cliff Richard's interest in Buddy. His own career has also developed along the lines that Buddy Holly had planned to follow—from song writer to record producer and music publisher.

From the eight hopefuls, the producers finally decided upon Paul Hipp, a 24-year-old actor born in Philadelphia, who has an uncanny likeness to Buddy Holly even without make-up.

'Buddy Holly was a great influence on my teens. I used to dance around my bedroom to his music,' Paul says, 'and I've been writing songs and fronting my own rock 'n' roll band, Paul Hipp and The Heroes, in New York for some years. Just before the show I worked with Carole King and got a taste of British audiences when we appeared at the Royal Albert Hall.'

Paul studied acting at the Herbert Berghoff Studio in New York and made his debut on the stage there in *Angel City*. He has also appeared in several films, including *Sticky Fingers* and *China Girl*, for which he wrote and performed the theme song, 'Midnight'.

'Getting the part was an exciting challenge,' he says. 'It was also very odd because Buddy died in a plane crash in Iowa and on the day of the last casting I heard on the news that there was a plane crash in Iowa.

'The show is like a big party, but my biggest moment was when Buddy's widow

brother, David, and called himself Teddy Jack Eddy. But it still wasn't long before those who caught the group's act in clubs at places like Redondo Beach, Topanga Canyon and Calabasas, began to realise just who the guitarist really was. Teddy Jack Eddy, a.k.a Gary Busey, was also a ghost from the 'Fifties . . .

Though Gary is perhaps now best known as an actor, he is a musician at heart—and a multi-talented one, at that—who acknowledges his fame to the shade of Buddy Holly. And, curiously, his struggle to make his mark as a musician was also uncannily like that of Holly—and there are those who feel his subsequent success in films mirrors what might well have awaited Buddy in Hollywood if he had not taken that fateful aeroplane ride.

Playing Buddy Holly on the screen as well as performing his music in public has not surprisingly given Gary a unique insight into the star, which in turn enables him to add his own contribution as to why the Holly legend has grown to such proportions.

At its most basic, Gary believes, the answer lies in the sound that Buddy Holly made. 'You can't beat that sound,' he says in the rolling tones of a Texan born and raised. 'You just can't beat that old rock 'n' roll the way Holly did it.'

The parallels between Gary's life and that of Buddy Holly began early. William Gary Busey was born in 1945, just to the east of Houston on the Galveston Bay in the Gulf of Mexico, at a little town called Goose Creek. (As Gary says, you won't find it on the map nowadays as the place has been renamed Bayton.)

Gary's father was a construction worker, which entailed regular moves to new sites, and while the boy was still young the family moved to Tulsa, Oklahoma. Here, when he was about ten, Gary was first introduced to rock music by a teenage neighbour. A little later he was given a small record player as a birthday present and the first discs he remembers buying were singles by Roy Orbison, Little Richard, Elvis Presley and Buddy Holly. His love of music also made him take up playing the drums.

Recalling these days, he says, 'I grew up listening to Buddy, Elvis and Roy Orbison. At first I wanted to be a rock 'n' roll star and that's what later took me to California.'

Gary's first taste of performing was actually in the Sheridan Avenue Christian Church in Tulsa. Then he graduated to singing in musical productions at Coffeyville Junior College, appearing in *South Pacific* and *Bye Bye, Birdie* (where he also met his future wife, Judy Helkenberg). Finally, rock grabbed him at Oklahoma State University when he joined a group called 'The Rubber Band', later re-christened 'Carp'.

'Carp' were an accomplished and popular group who gradually spread their net from performing locally to touring in the South and playing dates in places such as Disneyland and Knotts Berry Farm. They also caught the ear of a talent scout from Epic Records and cut an album for the label.

In 1968, Gary finished college, gave up music temporarily, and moved to Los Angeles to become a student of the actor-writer-teacher, James Best, who has remained his mentor ever since. Gary moved as naturally into acting as he had done playing music, and after parts in a number of TV series, graduated to movies in Roger Corman's *Angels Hard As They Come* (1970), following this with parts in *The Last American Hero*, *Thunderbolt and Lightfoot*, and a leading role as Kris Kristofferson's road manager in *A Star is Born* (1976).

It was in that same year of 1976 that his life was—as he admits—irrevocably changed when he took on the personality of Buddy Holly.

Opposite: 'A ghost from the 'Fifties'—Gary Busey as the star of *The Buddy Holly Story*, made in 1978.

'Of course, I knew all about Buddy Holly, but I was still a bit surprised when these three guys approached me to play him,' Gary recalls, 'not the least because I was 33 years old—eleven years older than Buddy when he died!'

The 'three guys' were the independent group of film makers, Ed Cohen, Fred Bauer and Steve Rash, who had just spent months persuading Maria Elena Holley to let them film her husband's life story after she had consistently turned down the approaches of several major studios who were interested in the same idea.

Gary had just finished making a film about surfing, *Big Wednesday*, for John Milius, with Jan-Michael Vincent and Billy Katt, when he approached his moment of destiny. He recalls the moment very clearly.

'I had just got out of 25-foot surf at Hawaii and come home—there was actually still salt brine on my arms! But they took me to the studios, cut my hair and curled it, and put on some glasses. I looked in the mirror—and, oh man!

'You know, I couldn't see Gary Busey any more. He just wasn't there. And I said to myself, "God damn! That is really throwing me off!"'

Instead of being 'thrown off', however, Gary drew on his love of rock 'n' roll and his acting talents to turn himself into the gangling young singer. Apart from the facial changes, he also had to shed pounds in weight.

'I just had to put myself there as a rock 'n' roll star, circa 1957, in Texas,' he goes on. 'And in order for me to believe I really *was* Buddy Holly, I had to commit myself one hundred per cent emotionally and do and say what would be natural.'

His task was not made any easier because of the scarcity of contemporary material about Buddy—there were some photographs, but perhaps most valuable of all some recently discovered TV film footage.

'Most of us never got a chance to see Buddy Holly in action,' Gary continues, 'and there are only a couple of film clips from television appearances in existence. But having seen this, you know, despite his appearance, Buddy was a raver!

'That's what I've heard, too. And watching the clip of him singing "Peggy Sue" on the Ed Sullivan Show, I was struck most of all by how effortless he was. Sure, he kept his right leg moving and he'd put his head back to accentuate a line, but he was planted in one spot. It was a revelation!'

That was not the only thing that surprised him about the character he was to play. 'Buddy was a strong character, though he may have looked like a weed. He did things his way. I heard he slugged the first record producer he ever had and walked out of Nashville.'

Gary says, in fact, that making the film was rather like going on a rock 'n' roll tour.

'I really got carried away in some of the music scenes. After each one it took me hours to wind down. It really depressed me when the music was over. I remember that the last musical scene we shot was the Ed Sullivan Show and Don Stroud who played my drummer was so upset that the band was going to break up. That's how much we were into it.'

Gary admits he felt a changed man at the end of making *The Buddy Holly Story*.

'After we had wrapped I went home and Judy opened the door. She said, "Welcome back." And I said, "I feel different. I feel as if I'm in a vacuum. When I look out of my eyes everything they see is different. I just don't know what it is."'

It was Gary's mentor, James Best, who explained to him what had happened.

'James said to me, "You have to watch out for the roles you play because

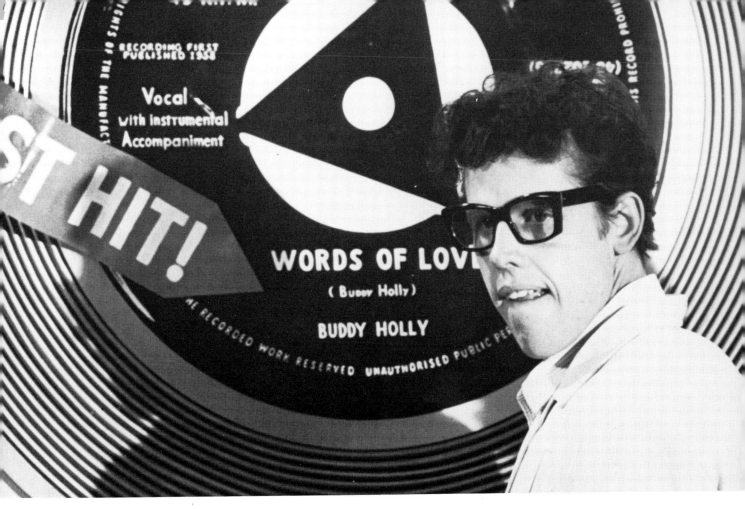

Gary Busey's performance as Holly gave his widow, Maria Elena, 'goose pimples—it seemed like Buddy was up there on the screen.'

they'll jump right into your real time." He was absolutely right—that was just what happened playing Buddy.'

As if in confirmation of this, Gary produces a letter he received from the wife of Niki Sullivan, who told him that his performance had convinced her children that Buddy Holly was something special. 'Now they have someone to relate to,' she wrote. 'All they had seen of Buddy Holly was a few pictures and they couldn't ever imagine him being the same age as their Daddy because he has gone. Since seeing the movie he will always be twenty-two to them.'

Gary also had a moving experience when he visited Lubbock on his way to Dallas for the premiere of the film. He had gone there ostensibly for publicity, but during his visit curiosity took him to see Buddy's grave and gave him the chance to meet the singer's parents, Lawrence and Ella.

'I have never felt so humble in my life as when I met Mr and Mrs Holley,' he recalls. 'Mrs Holley just started talking to me as if I was her boy. Her attitude really touched me—it was as if we had known each other for years.

'She also took me into Buddy's room in their house. It is full of his records and guitars and there are photographs of him round the walls. It's a bit like a shrine.

'And while we were standing there, I took down Buddy's Gibson and played a few lines of "Heartbeat" adding a bit of lullaby scatting between the lines. And when I looked at Mrs Holley she said, "Honey, I think your G-string's just a little bit flat!"

'I didn't know what to say or think. There I was getting all emotional and making it a bigger thing than it was and she just brought me right back down to earth. Just like any mother would.'

117

The visit to Buddy's grave proved an even more traumatic experience for Gary.

'I can still see every detail of that grave in my mind today. I can feel it on my hand now—and as I stood there I felt like I was looking at my own grave. It was very weird!'

Gary was introduced to Buddy's widow at the film's premiere in Dallas. She told him, 'It seemed like Buddy was up there on the screen. I had goose pimples and was shaking all the way through. You came through so vividly.'

Gary is honest enough to admit, however, that the film is not totally true to the facts of Buddy's life. (A copy of the storyline is reproduced at the end of this section.)

'It's really the legend of Buddy Holly,' he says candidly. 'We made some things bigger than life and took some licence to show the scope of his life.'

Despite this licence, *The Buddy Holly Story* was widely acclaimed as a wonderful evocation of the young singer's life. Film critic Andrew Sarris, for one, was quite unequivocal in his praise: 'Gary Busey seems to have lost so much weight that the shape of his head has changed, and he looks every inch the lead. I cannot recall another performer in the history of the cinema who has altered his screen image so drastically and dynamically in such a short space of time.'

Gary's performance won him more than just praise. He was nominated for both an Oscar and a Golden Globe Award, and named Best Actor of the Year by the National Society of Film Critics. (The film did win *one* Oscar for the Best Original Song Score—a tribute that Buddy himself would surely have been proud of!)

In the time since the film was released only one prominent dissenting voice has been heard—that of Norman Petty.

'I never felt I was looking at Buddy Holly,' the record producer told British journalist, Nina Myskow. 'And I've received a number of phone calls from people quite surprised that a film supposedly about Buddy's life should not mention the man who produced his hit records!'

For his part, Gary Busey has made further movies since *The Buddy Holly Story*, as well as continuing to play occasionally with the Old Dog Band. But he knows beyond any shadow of a doubt that he, too, is now a part of the Buddy Holly legend—and destined to remain so.

If there is anything other than pleasure at this association, Gary gives no hint of it. He merely says, 'My biggest get-off in life is playing live music. That's why you'll find me playing those little saloons.'

The Ghost of Buddy Holly plays on . . .

THE BUDDY HOLLY STORY
A SYNOPSIS

Lubbock, Texas. Live from the Parker Roller Rink, KDAV Radio broadcast the 'Holly Hayride'—Buddy Holly on guitar, Jesse Clarence on drums and Ray Bob Simms on double bass. In the middle of their programme the boys introduce one of Buddy's own tunes, 'That'll Be The Day'. It is received with wild enthusiasm by the teenage skaters, but to the consternation of KDAV owner Riley Randolph a riot breaks out and the show has to be taken off the air.

When the local newspaper runs a headline denouncing the event, Buddy becomes dispirited. He then hears from a record executive who was in town on the night of the broadcast and is invited to record a demo tape in Nashville. The session is not successful, and things look even blacker when the radio sponsors announce their dislike of Holly's music and cancel any further appearances.

Riley Randolph, however, personally admires the new sound and sends a recording of the radio programme to Coral Records. Buddy, Jesse and Ray Bob are rehearsing in a garage when a strange call comes through from a radio disc jockey in New York. Locked in the station's control room he is attempting to break the record of 24 hours non-stop disc playing by airing 'That'll Be The Day' which, unknown to Holly, has been released as a single record. During the excitement of the phone call a cricket starts chirping in the garage and as Buddy explains the strange sound the DJ thinks that he is being told the name of the backing group. He announces over the radio that the name of the group is Buddy Holly and The Crickets.

Buddy Holly and the boys go to New York for a meeting with Coral Records executive, Ross Turner. On accepting Buddy's stipulation that the group control their own recording sessions, a contract is signed and Ross predicts a great future for Buddy Holly and The Crickets. Buddy is also delighted to meet Turner's secretary, Maria Elena Santiago, and becomes very much attracted to her.

In error the group are booked to play the all-black Apollo Theatre in New York. When they arrive at the theatre the manager is thoroughly shaken to be confronted by a white group, but when they go on stage the black audience loves them and the show is a fabulous success.

While based in New York, Buddy and Maria Elena develop their relationship and with the blessing of Maria's aunt they marry and set up home. With Buddy now settled down the group pursue a hectic show business life, but Jesse and Ray Bob grow increasingly homesick for Lubbock. Buddy and the two boys agree to part and after a period of producing other acts, Buddy decides to go on the road again as a solo performer. Maria encourages him in this, but being three months pregnant she is sad to see him leave on a long tour.

The winter tour has on the same bill as Buddy, Ritchie Valens, saxophonist King Curtis and J.P. 'The Big Bopper' Richardson. When their bus breaks down in Clear Lake, Iowa, Buddy hires a small private plane to take him on to the next engagement.

In the early hours of 3 February, 1959, Buddy Holly dies when that chartered plane crashes at Mason City, Iowa. He is only 22.

*   *   *

THE BUDDY HOLLY SONGS PLAYED IN THE MOVIE: Rock Around With Ollie Vee, That'll Be The Day, Peggy Sue, Rave On, Oh Boy!, It's So Easy, Words of Love, Maybe Baby, Listen To Me, Every Day, True Love Ways, Well All Right.

Listen to Me

Buddy Holly wrote all his famous songs against a background of three dramatic years of history—yet despite any influence contemporary events may have had on his compositions, they have remained timeless and fresh to this day. He also wrote a number of other tunes which were never published or performed during his lifetime and have only recently come to light—providing an opportunity I have taken to include some details about them in this final chapter of my book.

Buddy crammed virtually all of his composing into the last three years of his life—indeed, he showed little interest in writing songs until 1956 when he was trying to break into the recording business. It was a year, though, when show business and national unrest competed for the headlines.

In America, Dr Martin Luther King was using 'passive resistance and the weapon of love' in the fight for black rights in the South, while in Europe the Hungarians rose up against Soviet rule and Colonel Nasser seized the Suez Canal from its Anglo-French owners. The Russians almost at once put down the revolt with savage brutality, while Anglo-French forces who stormed into Egypt were forced to pull out as a result of pressure by the United Nations. In show business, *My Fair Lady* with Rex Harrison and Julie Andrews opened in New York in March, just a few weeks ahead of John Osborne's ground-breaking drama *Look Back In Anger* in London; the following month Nat King Cole was dragged from a stage in Alabama while singing to a white audience; and in June in Britain playwright Arthur Miller married Marilyn Monroe.

The September newspapers were full of stories of Teddy Boys in Britain rioting during showings of the film *Rock Around The Clock* starring Bill Haley, while in the USA Elvis Presley was seen by approximately 82 per cent of the TV viewing

Kathleen Turner playing the girl 'in just about every song', Peggy Sue, in the 1986 film, *Peggy Sue Got Married*.

population when he appeared on the Ed Sullivan Show. His performance of 'Hound Dog' that night was described by one critic as 'looking as if he was sneering with his legs'.

Of Buddy's four songs recorded in 1956, 'Blue Days, Black Nights', 'Love Me', 'Modern Don Juan' and 'You Are My One Desire', none really hinted at the creativity to follow. But in the autumn, Buddy and Jerry Allison saw the new John Ford Western, *The Searchers*, and got the inspiration for what was to prove their first big hit, 'That'll Be The Day'.

Both young men were as deeply impressed by *The Searchers* as the critics had been. Indeed, this Western film, about two men who spend five years in primitive country searching for a young girl who has been captured by Indians, was described by one writer as 'sublime' and it is now firmly established as a classic. John Wayne's performance as Ethan Edwards is almost mythic in its intensity, and Buddy and Jerry sat enraptured in the stalls of their local cinema as Big John pursued his vengeance against the Comanche raiders. But what stuck most firmly in their minds was a phrase that Wayne used whenever he disagreed with anyone. 'That'll be the day!' he would scowl. After Buddy and Jerry left the cinema, they began using the words as a catch phrase and from this evolved the idea for the song—recorded the following year—which similarly embodied the same kind of toughness and cynicism that John Wayne had expressed. (Buddy later rather incongruously utilised a second catch phrase, Little Richard's 'Well All Right', for the title of a gentle love song he released in 1958.)

Another catch phrase became a national craze in Britain in January 1957 when Bill Haley and the Comets arrived for a tour. 'See you later alligator' were the words from one of their songs, with the response, 'In a while crocodile'. Haley told reporters that the secret of rock 'n' roll's success was its simplicity: 'Everyone wants to get into the act. With rock 'n' roll they can join in.' On the world scene, San Francisco was hit by its worst earthquake since the big one in 1906; British Prime Minister Harold Macmillan coined the phrase, 'never had it so good'; and the Russians inaugurated the space age by launching a dog called Laika into orbit in a satellite. As the year closed, British newspapers claimed that 'British rock 'n' rollers fight US invasion' as Tommy Steele, Marty Wilde and Lonnie Donegan broke into the pop charts.

Apart from 'That'll Be The Day', 1957 produced several more Holly classics —'I'm Looking For Someone To Love' (complete with yet another saying Buddy had borrowed, Mrs Holley's 'drunk man, street car, foot slip, there you are!'); 'Words of Love' in which Buddy sang with himself in one of the earliest examples of double tracking; and 'Everyday' in which the unique pitter-patter rhythm was achieved by Jerry Allison tapping out the beat on his jean-clad thighs instead of using his drums. And, of course, 'Peggy Sue'—arguably one of the most influential of all his compositions.

There are several versions as to how Buddy created this unforgettable love song. The most generally accepted is that the tune was originally named 'Cindy Lou' after Buddy's young niece, but while the three Crickets were rehearsing the number, Jerry Allison asked if it could be changed to 'Peggy Sue' after his current girlfriend. Buddy had no objections—and despite an initial problem with the first take of the record when Allison—of all people!—got the name wrong and there was a debate as to whether it should revert to the old title, 'Peggy Sue' it became and has remained.

But for this change of title the question has to be asked whether the song would have proved so influential. Would 'Cindy Lou' have found her way onto other songs like Bobby Darin's 'Splish Splash' and 'Queen of the Hop', and Ritchie Valen's 'Ooh My Head'? And, most importantly of all, would she have inspired the great line, 'You recall a girl that's been in nearly every song,' for one of Buddy's last songs, 'Peggy Sue Got Married', which he put on tape in New York in January 1959, and which later still inspired the Kathleen Turner film? Incidentally, this sequel, title and all, had been suggested to Buddy by his father.

The importance of Lawrence Holley in his son's career has not been given full recognition according to Norman Petty. Talking in the early 1980s, shortly before his death from leukaemia, The Crickets' mentor said, 'Buddy's father is the real hero of the Buddy Holly story. He was the man who gave Buddy his tremendous strength. Buddy knew he had his Dad's backing in *everything* he did.'

Another interesting footnote to the song is that Jerry Allison did marry Peggy Sue but the marriage failed and the couple parted—though no one as yet has chosen to add this finale to the legend . . .

On 6 February, 1958, almost exactly a year to the day before Buddy's fatal plane accident, an airliner crashed in dreadful wintry conditions at Munich airport in Germany, killing eight members of the famous Manchester United 'Busby Babes' football team. In March, the Americans followed the Russians into space, launching their first satellite, Explorer—although such headlines were soon put to one side when Elvis sacrificed his famous sideburns to join the US Army and do his two years' service.

In May, Buddy's friend Jerry Lee Lewis ran foul of the British Press and establishment when it was revealed during his tour that he was accompanied by a 13-year-old wife. The planned five-week tour was at once abandoned after just two concerts. The continuing clashes between police and Teddy Boys resulted in 35 youths being charged in Nottingham in August, and this was followed by the first race riots to be experienced in Britain in London's Notting Hill Gate in September, when petrol bombs were thrown at the police and 59 people were arrested. For those who were interested in innovations, the Radio Show introduced the first stereo or hi-fi system for record lovers, and car enthusiasts saw the first German-manufactured 'Bubble-cars' at the Motor Show.

'Maybe Baby', which was released in February 1958, is sometimes referred to as one of the most unusual of Buddy's songs—a fact perhaps explained because it was mostly written by his mother! Talking about her involvement with her son in his songwriting, Mrs Ella Holley said at the premiere of *The Buddy Holly Story*, 'We were behind Buddy one hundred per cent. We were very anxious for him to make a career as a singer. We were his biggest fans.

'You know, I wrote "Maybe Baby" for Buddy. I was always trying to help him write and he always said my songs were too serious. So I decided I would write him a silly one. I wrote "Maybe Baby" and gave it to him and the next thing I knew it was out on a record. I said, "I hope you didn't put my name on it?" And he said, "Oh, no, I knew better than that!"'

Buddy later repaid this debt by recording one of Mrs Holley's favourite songs, the old music hall standard, 'Wait Till The Sun Shines Nellie'—though his arrangement was so far from the original that her opinion of the disc can only be guessed at!

Buddy's last year also saw the release of 'Rave On', 'Think It Over', 'It's So Easy' and 'Heartbeat', all of which have played their respective parts in ensuring his unique place in the annals of rock. Then came the strangely appropriate final release before his death, 'It Doesn't Matter Anymore' which, though it was written by Paul Anka, was eerily reminiscent of the last record by Buddy's first hero, Hank Williams, entitled 'I'll Never Get Out Of This World Alive'.

Inevitably, there was much left unsung and unpublished when Buddy died. But what he might have produced subsequently but for that plane journey on 3 February—only a few days after Fidel Castro had proclaimed himself the new ruler of Cuba, and one of the moguls of Hollywood, Cecil B. de Mille, had gone to his last rest—is now purely conjecture. Nevertheless, a little batch of his unpublished compositions came on view in April 1990 in London at an auction of rock memorabilia, and though few of them can be considered anywhere near complete—and all are without melodies—they make for interesting reading.

Several of the numbers are scribbled on the back of odd scraps of paper, indicating that once Buddy had an idea he immediately wrote it down on anything to hand. For instance, a tune called 'What You Gonna Do?' is written in blue ball-point pen on the back of a 'City of Lubbock Utility Bill' dated 4 February, 1957; while 'I Can Sing A Modern Lullaby' is dashed off in blue ink on some 'Weaver Airline Stationery' and 'Roll 'Em Up, Honey' on the back of a 1956 'City and School Tax Notice' addressed to his father!

Just how widely Buddy's musical interests ranged can be judged by studying the lyrics for an out-and-out rocker like 'Hit And Run Lover' and two love ballads, 'Side By Side With The Girl I Love' and 'My Sugar', and then a moving religious song, 'After Having Met My Saviour', written some time in 1958. There is also something of a sense of premonition about the twenty lines of lyrics which make up 'Heartbreak Tomorrow'.

Anyone glancing at these manuscript sheets would have wondered, as I did, what might have been the outcome if the young author had got round to finishing 'Monetta', another song in the 'Peggy Sue' tradition. For there is something full of promise about the 30 existing lines which begin: 'Monetta—I—Betta—I Getta—Sweet Kisses from you . . .' Perhaps equally intriguing is another sheet containing nine lines in blue ball-point, which almost reads like a forerunner of a Beatles' classic: 'I saw her standing there . . .'

However, one manuscript more than any other caught my eye and stopped me in my tracks. For several of Buddy's published songs have, of course, been suggested as his epitaph: 'Not Fade Away' and 'Rave On', to name but two. But here was another song of fifteen lines written on blue lined notepaper and clearly amongst the earlier of his efforts at composition. It was entitled rather prosaically 'My Blue Eyed Sweetie Pie' and did not strike me as remarkable until I reached the last line. For there were ten words which so aptly summed up The Legend That Is Buddy Holly—written by the man himself.

'There's been a lot of talk since I left town . . .'

BUDDY HOLLY: A DISCOGRAPHY

Singles

BLUE DAYS BLACK NIGHTS/LOVE ME (July 1956)	Brunswick 05581
THAT'LL BE THE DAY/I'M LOOKING FOR SOMEONE TO LOVE (by The Crickets, September 1957)	Vogue Coral Q 72279
PEGGY SUE/EVERYDAY (November 1957)	Vogue Coral Q 72293
OH BOY/NOT FADE AWAY (by The Crickets, December 1957)	Coral Q 72298
THAT'LL BE THE DAY/I'M LOOKING FOR SOMEONE TO LOVE (by The Crickets; January 1958)	Coral Q 72279
PEGGY SUE/EVERYDAY (January 1958)	Coral Q 72293
LISTEN TO ME/I'M GONNA LOVE YOU TOO (February 1958)	Coral Q 72288
MAYBE BABY/TELL ME HOW (by The Crickets, February 1958)	Coral Q 72307
RAVE ON/TAKE YOUR TIME (June 1958)	Coral Q 72325
THINK IT OVER/FOOL'S PARADISE (by The Crickets; July 1958)	Coral Q 72329
EARLY IN THE MORNING/NOW WE'RE ONE (August 1958)	Coral Q 72333
IT'S SO EASY/LONESOME TEARS (by The Crickets; October 1958)	Coral Q 72345

HEARTBEAT/WELL ALL RIGHT (November 1958)	Coral Q 72346
IT DOESN'T MATTER ANYMORE/RAINING IN MY HEART (February 1959)	Coral Q 72360
MIDNIGHT SHIFT/ROCK AROUND WITH OLLIE VEE (June 1959)	Brunswick 05800
PEGGY SUE GOT MARRIED/CRYING WAITING HOPING (August 1959)	Coral Q 72376
HEARTBEAT/EVERYDAY (March 1960)	Coral Q 72392
TURE LOVE WAYS/MOONDREAMS (May 1960)	Coral Q 72397
LEARNING THE GAME/THAT MAKES IT TOUGH (October 1960)	Coral Q 72411
WHAT TO DO/THAT'S WHAT THEY SAY (January 1961)	Coral Q 72419
BABY I DON'T CARE/VALLEY OF TEARS (June 1961)	Coral Q 72432
LOOK AT ME/MAILMAN BRING ME NO MORE BLUES (November 1961)	Coral Q 72445
LISTEN TO ME/WORDS OF LOVE (February 1962)	Coral Q 72449
REMINISCING/WAIT TILL THE SUN SHINES NELLIE (September 1962)	Coral Q 72455
BROWN EYED HANDSOME MAN/SLIPPIN' & SLIDIN' (March 1963)	Coral Q 72459
BO DIDDLEY/IT'S NOT MY FAULT (May 1963)	Coral Q 72463
WISHING/BECAUSE I LOVE YOU (August 1963)	Coral Q 72466
WHAT TO DO/UMM OH YEAH (DEAREST) (December 1963)	Coral Q 72469
YOU'VE GOT LOVE/AN EMPTY CUP (April 1964)	Coral Q 72472
LOVE'S MADE A FOOL OF YOU/YOU'RE THE ONE (September 1964)	Coral Q 72475
MAYBE BABY/THAT'S MY DESIRE (May 1966)	Coral Q 72483
PEGGY SUE/RAVE ON (March 1968)	MCA MU 1012
OH BOY/THAT'LL BE THE DAY (by The Crickets with Buddy Holly, May 1968)	MCA MU 1017
LOVE IS STRANGE/YOU'RE THE ONE (January 1969)	MCA MU 1059
IT DOESN'T MATTER ANYMORE/MAYBE BABY (May 1969)	MCA MU 1081
RAVE ON/UMM OH YEAH (DEAREST) (March 1970)	MCA MU 1116
THAT'LL BE THE DAY/WELL ALL RIGHT/EVERYDAY (May 1973)	MCA MMU 1198
IT DOESN'T MATTER ANYMORE/TRUE LOVE WAYS/BROWN EYED HANDSOME MAN (February 1974)	MCA 119
OH BOY/EVERYDAY (by Buddy Holly & The Crickets, August 1975)	MCA 207
TRUE LOVE WAYS/IT DOESN'T MATTER ANYMORE/ RAINING IN MY HEART/MOONDREAMS (September 1976)	MCA 252
PEGGY SUE/RAVE ON/ROCK AROUND WITH OLLIE VEE/MIDNIGHT SHIFT (September 1976)	MCA 253
MAYBE BABY/THINK IT OVER/THAT'LL BE THE DAY/IT'S SO EASY (by Buddy Holly & The Crickets, September 1976)	MCA 254
WISHING/LOVE'S MADE A FOOL OF YOU (January 1978)	MCA 344

THAT'LL BE THE DAY/I'M LOOKING FOR SOMEONE TO
LOVE (by The Crickets, July 1982)   Old Gold OG 9208
PEGGY SUE/EVERYDAY (July 1982)   Old Gold OG 9222
OH BOY/NOT FADE AWAY (by The Crickets, July 1982) Old Gold OG 9223
MAYBE BABY/TELL ME HOW (by The Crickets,
July 1983)   Old Gold OG 9224
RAVE ON/TRUE LOVE WAYS (April 1983)   Old Gold OG 9319
IT DOESN'T MATTER ANYMORE/RAINING IN MY HEART
(April 1983)   Old Gold OG 9325
THAT'LL BE THE DAY/ROCK ME MY BABY (August 1985) MCA BH 1
PEGGY SUE/EVERYDAY (August 1985)   MCA BH 2
OH BOY/NOT FADE AWAY (August 1985)   MCA BH 3
MAYBE BABY/TELL ME HOW (August 1985)   MCA BH 4
RAVE ON/READY TEDDY (August 1985)   MCA BH 5
THINK IT OVER/IT'S SO EASY (August 1985)   MCA BH 6
IT DOESN'T MATTER ANYMORE/RAINING IN MY HEART
(August 1985)   MCA BH 7
TRUE LOVE WAYS/WORDS OF LOVE (August 1985)   MCA BH 8
REMINISCING/BABY I DON'T CARE (August 1985) MCA BH 9
BROWN EYED HANDSOME MAN/BO DIDDLEY
(August 1985)   MCA BH 10
THAT'LL BE THE DAY/I'M LOOKING FOR SOMEONE TO
LOVE (August 1986)   MCA THAT 1
THAT'LL BE THE DAY/I'M LOOKING FOR SOMEONE TO
LOVE/IT DOESN'T MATTER ANYMORE/RAINING IN MY
HEART (August 1986)   MCA THATT 1

Extended Plays

BUDDY HOLLY (September 1958)   Coral FEP 2002
THE SOUND OF THE CRICKETS (by The Crickets,
September 1958)   Coral FEP 2003
RAVE ON (December 1958)   Coral FEP 2005
IT'S SO EASY (by The Crickets, January 1959) Coral FEP 2014
HEARTBEAT (January 1959)   Coral FEP 2015
THE BUDDY HOLLY STORY (June 1959)   Coral FEP 2032
BUDDY HOLLY NO. 1 (July 1959)   Brunswick OE 9456
BUDDY HOLLY NO. 2 (July 1959)   Brunswick OE 9457
THE LATE GREAT BUDDY HOLLY (February 1960)   Coral FEP 2044
FOUR MORE BY THE CRICKETS (by The Crickets,
May 1960)   Coral FEP 2060
THAT'LL BE THE DAY (by The Crickets,
November 1960)   Coral FEP 2062
BUDDY—BY REQUEST (September 1964)   Coral FEP 2065
THAT TEX-MEX SOUND (September 1964)   Coral FEP 2066
WISHING (October 1964)   Coral FEP 2067
SHOWCASE VOL. 1 (November 1964)   Coral FEP 2068
SHOWCASE VOL. 2 (November 1964)   Coral FEP 2069
BUDDY HOLLY SINGS (January 1965)   Coral FEP 2070

Albums

THE CHIRPING CRICKETS (by The Crickets; March 1958) — Coral LVA 9081

BUDDY HOLLY (July 1958) — Coral LVA 9085

THE BUDDY HOLLY STORY (April 1959) — Coral LVA 9105

THE BUDDY HOLLY STORY VOL. 2 (November 1960) — Coral LVA 9127

THAT'LL BE THE DAY (October 1961) — Ace Of Hearts AH 3

REMINISCING (April 1963) — Coral LVA 9212

SHOWCASE (June 1964) — Coral LVA 9222

HOLLY IN THE HILLS (June 1965) — Coral LVA 9227

HOLLY IN THE HILLS (July 1965) — Coral LVA 9227

BUDDY HOLLY'S GREATEST HITS (June 1967) — Ace Of Hearts AH 148

LISTEN TO ME (July 1968) — MCA MUP 312

RAVE ON (July 1968) — MCA MUP 313

BROWN EYED HANDSOME MAN (July 1968) — MCA MUP 314

HE'S THE ONE (July 1968) — MCA MUP 315

TRUE LOVE WAYS (July 1968) — MCA MUP 319

WISHING (July 1968) — MCA MUP 320

GIANT (February 1969) — MCA MUPS 371

BUDDY HOLLY'S GREATEST HITS (November 1969) — Coral CP 8

THE CHIRPING CRICKETS (by The Crickets, December 1969) — Coral CP 20

THAT'LL BE THE DAY (December 1969) — Coral CP 24

BUDDY HOLLY'S GREATEST HITS VOL. 2 (May 1970) — Coral CP 47

REMEMBER (September 1971) — Coral CPS 71

GREATEST HITS (February 1974) — Coral CRL 1001

GREATEST HITS VOL. 2 (February 1974) — Coral CRL 1005

THE CHIRPING CRICKETS (by The Crickets, February 1974) — Coral CRL 1023

THAT'LL BE THE DAY (February 1974) — Coral CRL 1024

REMEMBER (February 1974) — Coral CRL 1087

LISTEN TO ME (February 1974) — MCA MCF 2613

RAVE ON (February 1974) — MCA MCF 2614

BROWN EYED HANDSOME MAN (February 1974) — MCA MCF 2615

TRUE LOVE WAYS (February 1974) — MCA MCF 2616

GIANT (February 1974) — MCA MCF 2625

LEGEND (October 1974, double album) — Coral CDMSP 802

GREATEST HITS (July 1975) — Coral CDLM 8007

BUDDY HOLLY (July 1975) — Coral CDLM 8034

THE CHIRPING CRICKETS (by The Crickets, July 1975) — Coral CDLM 8035

RAVE ON (August 1975) — MFP 50176

THE BUDDY HOLLY STORY (5-LP boxed set, November 1975) — World Records SM 301/5

THE NASHVILLE SESSIONS (November 1975) — Coral CDLM 8038

WESTERN AND BOP (November 1977) — Coral CDLM 8055

20 GOLDEN GREATS (February 1978) — EMI EMTV 8

THE COMPLETE BUDDY HOLLY (6-LP boxed set,
March 1979)   Coral CDLM 807
20 GOLDEN GREATS (June 1979)   MCA MCTV 1
HEARTBEAT (August 1980)   M & S IMP 114
BUDDY HOLLY (September 1970)   Pickwick SSP 3070
ROCK WITH BUDDY HOLLY (October 1980)   MFP 50490
LOVE SONGS (August 1981)   MCA MCF 3117
GREATEST HITS (September 1981)   MCA MCC 1618
LEGEND (March 1982, double LP)   MCA/Coral MCLD
                                                     606
20 LOVE SONGS (August 1982)   MFP 5570
FOR THE FIRST TIME ANYWHERE (March 1983)   MCA MCM 1002
BUDDY HOLLY (March 1983)   MCA MCL 1752
THE CHIRPING CRICKETS (by The Crickets;
March 1983)   MCA MCL 1753
THE NASHVILLE SESSIONS (March 1983)   MCA MCL 1754
23 ALL TIME GREATEST HITS (November 1984)   Astan 20125
BUDDY HOLLY ROCKS (May 1985, double LP)   Charly CDX 8
GOLDEN GREATS (July 1985)   MCA MCM 5003
FROM THE ORIGINAL MASTER TAPES (1986)   MCA DIDX 20
SOMETHING SPECIAL FROM BUDDY HOLLY
(September 1986)   Rollercoaster
                                                     ROLL 2013
THE BEST OF BUDDY HOLLY (September 1986)   Hallmark
                                                     SHM 3199

ROCK AROUND WITH BUDDY HOLLY & THE CRICKETS
(September 1986, double LP)   Cambra CR 123
REMINISCING (November 1986)   MCA MCL 1824
SHOWCASE (November 1986)   MCA MCL 1825
GIANT (November 1986)   MCA MCL 1826
THE LEGENDARY BUDDY HOLLY (October 1987)   Hallmark
                                                     SHM 3221
ROCK'N'ROLL GREATS (October 1987)   MFP 5806
BUDDY HOLLY (October 1987, double album)   Castle CCSLP 172
THE COMPLETE BUDDY HOLLY (November 1988,
6-LP Album)   MCA CDSP 807
THE UNFORGETTABLE BUDDY (October 1989)   Reader's Digest
                                                     301760

Buddy's number one UK fan, Ray Needham, proud owner of a vast collection of Holly recordings.